God, Please Tie My Shoes

By Dr. Rebecca Foster

Contents

First Edition August 2019

Author: Dr. Rebecca Foster

Book Design by Dr. Rebecca Foster
Illustrations by Brianna Sutton & Dr. Rebecca Foster
Graphics by Bradley Foster
Editor: A. Fox
ISBN: Paperback

Published by KDP

SPECIAL THANKS

To my editor A. Fox for helping me to clarify my thoughts and words for readers.

To Brianna Sutton, thank you for taking on the task of drawing the images I presented to you even though you were finishing up your degree. I thank you for your talent, and I hope you continue to use and grow it!!!

Thank you to my son, Bradley Foster, for using your photographic genius to complete my cover.

I thank Kim Borders for being such a good friend, helping me to figure this gift out better, and find my direction. Thank you.

I thank my family for always standing by me, growing with me as I develop my gift and reach out to the world. I love you all for understanding the need for me to share my messages and knowledge with others and walk with me as I do as God directs me. Thank you to my husband Brian for choosing to rise with me as I climb blindly. Thank you for trusting me.

Thank you to the readers, because without you this book would not mean anything.

Dedicated to God and all the wonders of this Universe that are

seen only with faith.

NOTE TO GOD

Father God, I sit here after several years of hearing Your voice tell me to write another book. So much has happened in the last 11 years since I published The Beaches that I just have not had the time or ambition to start. You know this to be true, as You have given me many other tasks to complete. Writing this book has been on my mind every day for years, and lately it seems that You have been prodding me more and more to write. I have repeatedly said to myself that I needed to remember specific messages from You, and to tell you the truth, I have not done so. I have hoped that I would remember what was needed to tell, and I also hope that You will help me write this book again. Funny thing is that when people tell me about a passage or portion of The Beaches that touched them, I must look it up, because I do not remember writing it. I am thankful for Your input, Your presence, and Your guidance as I attempt to write this next chapter. I could not be here without You; I would not be here without you in so many ways. I need You; I love You, and I always seek You. Thank You for entrusting me with such a gift. I hope I make You proud as I attempt to follow Your lead.

PREFACE

Understand that regardless of identity, you are you; however, I am going to use Mary or Joe as examples, and respective He or She pronouns in each example. I understand that some may not identify as such, but I must write something and so I choose the basics. This is the second book in my journey of helping others, with the first being The Beaches: A Journey of Answers. In that book, I described how I read people, how they too can connect and understand God-given gifts better, and how readings relate to daily lives. In this book I go deeper into how God and Spirit works in our lives from beginning to end. I explain what I have been shown regarding suicide, angels and demons, humankind, and how we can make the most out of our time here on Earth. In this book I attempt to clarify and simplify the amazing relationship we have with Father God and how He works in our lives, as well as what we are meant to accomplish while here. I hope you enjoy this quick read, and I truly hope it brings discernment and light where there was once indifference and darkness.

Also, to answer the questions about why I would price my book so low is quite simple. If I had gone with a traditional publisher, I would have had to charge according to pages or design and that would increase the price. I looked at many avenues, and in order to do what I needed to do, I had to go with a company that would allow me to give my book away when possible. As I was stating before, I had a conversation with a person who inspired me in so many ways, and just previously, I had done several readings for individuals with autism. One of the readings had to be done over Skype, because the person I was reading for could only understand the reading visually. This led me to realize the same thing about how people learn, as some read, some have to have hands-on, and some need to see something. I wanted to ensure that this book was understood on many levels, hence the video links in the e-book.

INTRODUCTION

Your hearing is muffled. You cannot understand what is being said or grasp where it is coming from; it is as if you have earplugs in and all you catch are the tones in the voices. Your vision is also blurry like opening your eyes underwater, and the feeling of sensory helplessness is upon you. You can make out lights and shadows, though, and you find that you are in an unknown place, surrounded by unknown energies; all you really make out is their glow and presence, which is strangely hued in red. A beeping sound that moves up and down in tandem with your heartbeat makes its presence known, and the swoosh sound your heart is making can be heard across a machine somewhere outside this space you are in. How did you get here?

The beeping machine is in a white room, with small shadows of grey around shelf corners. One can just make out a large cupboard made of pressed wood against the wall. Light creeps in the half-closed curtains to the left, and although it is bright, it is not enough yet to reveal the room. Temperatures fluctuate from hot to cold as the air conditioning turns on and off, causing chills and sweats all in the same hours. A silver table sits next to the bed; it holds ice chips and a cup with a red-tinted popsicle stick standing half out of it. A table with a clear, plastic bin sits to the right against the wall, next to another table with a blue paper blanket folded neatly on top, holding sterile, stainless steel instruments, that, to be honest, look quite primitive. Bustling is heard out in the hallway to the right, as a nurse runs by saying, "Room 7 is about to deliver, call the doctor!"

It is your birthday, and many unknown things are happening around your mother as your life gets started. Your mother is focused on bringing a person into this world, the medical team is concerned with your health and safety, and Spirit is set upon ensuring your success, spiritual growth, and health. During this process of entering the Earthly plane, God removes the 'cheat sheet' that enables you to see your pasts, your current, and your future. It would be no fun to know all, all of the time. We are here to learn about others, as well as ourselves; knowing how to handle situations, both good and bad, are what build our character and soul. Knowing how to win all the battles, get the Boss, and end the game would be fruitless, and you would learn nothing; therefore, the memory of who you are is wiped clean, and you start this journey blindly in more ways than one. As I stated, humans and heavenly entities are not the only ones with a stake in your life. Many energies, celestial and angelic, as well as darker angels and demonic entities are all around the hospital, all of whom play a role in each new human's life. No one is even aware of the wrestling and war that is taking place already.

On a personal, Earthly level, you feel pressure and movement, security and love all at the same time. You are warm, protected, enveloped in light, yet caught between the heavenly place you call home and the Earthly place that is beckoning you towards it. You hear a chorus of familiar voices whisper, "Do not worry. We are all here. We always will be. Remember us." You know these voices, they are loving and special, and intimate. The concert of loving voices fades as you move through this tunnel. The next thing you know, you are pulled into a cold new world. A pair of hands grip you firmly, as you scream loudly, whaling your arrival into this dimension.

A woman in a blue shirt cleans you off. You are blinded by the lights and screaming incoherently. Some of you are even upset to be back, which makes it that much worse! (We will discuss that later....) Your recognition of those last few angelic words, selectively erased from your conscious memory. You are now in a human shell; it is constricting and cold, leaving you shivering and uncertain. These beings are all around you, checking you, measuring you, counting things, and making sure you are breathing properly. Someone is holding a piece of chilly metal to your chest. Closer now, you hear mumbling, and you are picked up and wrapped in a warm blanket. The rest is a blur as it all happens so quickly, and you find yourself lying in someone's arms. You hear the distant whispers, "Your Heavenly Father loves you," and then closer you hear, "Your mommy loves you so much." You get the picture. You are born an unknowing, helpless little human, with this magnificent and amazing soul comparable to the humans around you, yet you are now a baby, possibly starting over again. A lot of times you are dealing with people who have forgotten their celestial and spiritual connections, which only makes the journey more difficult. Time to wake up.

This is what I have been shown in all the years that I have been reading for people. It sounds so simple, yet it is very complex, mostly due to humans making it that way. Everyone wants to be different, but everyone wants to belong as well. Part of the issue is that people base most decisions on status, appearance, wealth, living situations, and who someone loves. Divides are created based on skin color, and political and religious affiliations. The fact of the matter is that we are all indeed different, but in so many ways we are the same. Humans are always trying to push their agendas of power on other humans, and when you do not ascribe to those agendas or beliefs, then you are cast out, which is stupid. Believe it or not, a person can believe in many different things all at the same time and still love God and be loved by God.

In these times, as it has been hundreds of years before, there is political and religious strife. Nothing will change until each Spiritual being, stuck in a human body, awakens to the fact that we are only temporarily here to learn about ourselves, others, and to improve this world. Only when that energy, that person, can become accepting, rather than tolerant of others, can we evolve into a better people…. a ONE people.

I am Rebecca Foster, a clairvoyant spiritual medium. I am clairvoyant, which means I see things clearly; I am spiritual and ground my work in faith, God, and Christ, and I am a medium, meaning I can see and hear the spirits of those who have passed over. They [God, Spirit Guides, and people passed over] also provide me with smells that those still living would know or recognize around a person when they were living, such as cookies, tar, or cigarette smoke. I have even smelled saltwater, fire, specific perfumes, and flowers. My information comes through symbolically and I interpret the messages. This is how my guides have taught me to understand them, and I have had people ask, "Why not just say the words instead of all the dumb symbols?" To hear a sentence is one thing, and we can take it at face value for what was said in terms of tone and words used; however, when I see a picture of a person standing on a beach, looking sadly across the horizon, with a broken boat in the water, I am given feeling, emotion, purpose, drive, reasoning, environment, as well as what has been, and should, or could be. I see it and then explain what it all means.

Being able to see in symbols with a gift of interpreting them opens me up to communicate not just with human, angelic, and divine souls and energies, but also those who cannot communicate verbally. Keep in mind, too, that as I am reading them, symbols may mean something significant to someone that may make absolutely no sense to me. I must admit that when this happens, I get "the chills," because it is a little inside message or joke between two people that wasn't meant for me. When people can say, "Rebecca, I know what they were showing you and here it is," I must admit, I am in awe, even after all the years of this gift.

My gift is not simply to aid those who are alive and verbal. I do love helping people when they need to talk to someone about something

and the person or animal, they need to talk to cannot communicate back.
As for communicating with the non-verbal, that would include animals,
both living and passed over, and communicating with those who are in a
coma, are high spectrum autism, or those who have dementia. This is
not something that always works depending on the soul and desire, or
availability of the soul, to talk with me. I want to be clear here that I am
not a magical being, I do not have supernatural powers, and I cannot just
make things happen. I can do none of this without God, as He is the One
who has provided me with my gift.

He is the One who guides me and sends angels to help me
communicate across the dimensions. His messages are meant to help
guide people in their current lives, bring up relevant past life information
that has a residual effect on current situations, and provide comfort and
reasoning to those who are struggling with current situations, such as
dealing with loss, or seeking for guidance. Another purpose for my
abilities is to confirm for some that they are on the right path, that they
are fulfilling their life's purpose, or that they are living according to
God's plan—even if they don't want to or don't believe it is possible.

People contact me to find out if they are heading the right course,
and to figure out what to do next, yet some simply want confirmation of

current situations. What is the right course? That is up to each individual.
I simply give up my ego and let things fall as they may. I trust that God
will put me where I need to be regardless if I wanted it or not. I have
found that hindsight is rich with information. I also base my walk on
how I feel. If I am nauseous, anxious, or simply feel ill over something, I
question my choices and actions. If I make corrections and that feeling
goes away, I know I made the right decision.

Sometimes I do not get the message, or it does not come through clearly,
and this is when God wants that person I am reading for to turn to Him
for the answers, or to delve deeper into themselves in order to gain more
self-confidence in their own decision-making abilities. I always direct
people to God first, to the writings to which they subscribe, or to the
bible. Some people want to know about relationships on both earthly and
spiritual planes; however, this is an area that I find is restricted to healing
old relationships and is less about finding new ones. Albeit, many times,
a person is shown new relationships they should watch out for in order to
transition to a new chapter in life. I do tend to stay away from questions
that involve finding a new love, or if one person is better for someone
than another. It tells me that they are not focusing on the right question;

rather, they should be asking, "What do I have to do to attract the right person? What do I need to fix in me first?"

People contact me to find out why they are depressed or why they suffer from anxiety. Reasons being they may have residual past life events hanging on them, or it could be more sinister, as in a darker energy connected to and tied to their energy. More and more people are awakening to their spiritual selves and leaving the earthly reasons for existence behind, which is another reason people are coming to me. It is quite amazing to read for someone who is here for others and not themselves, who is transitioning from earthly possessions and desire, and who acts more from the mind rather than the brain.

Imagine being blind to whom you truly are all your life. Keep in mind a life is complex, made up of purpose, reason, residue from past lives, and a current life contract, and when one awakens to these things, it can cause many questions to come up. People start seeing the coincidences, the happenings, the numbers, such

This is a vision of a woman who feels held back by external forces

(people and situations) and feels that opportunities are out of reach;

however, God does not dangle carrots. He puts us in situations to

challenge ourselves and grow. This represents all that she is capable

of.... even in a skirt.

as 11:11, 111, 222, 333, etc.; recurring signs, foreknowledge that comes to pass, and déjà vu may occur, leading people to think they are losing their minds. There are believers and non-believers, and both types of people come to me for readings. Some humans are very content in their Earthly lives, eyes on the ground, all happens as they make it happen, and all scientific ("Show me; prove it!"), yet they remain open to new thoughts and ideas, while keeping their feet firmly planted. But when these skeptics, or Earth-Bounders, as I like to call them, come to me for the first time, they arrive cautiously and end up leaving with possibility. Earth-Bounders are the best to read, because it gives me a chance to turn a person's way of thinking around and awaken another soul.

First, thank you for taking the time to get this far. My hope is that it will open you up to new thoughts, confirm what you are going through, or bring understanding about someone you love and what they may be going through as well. My entire life's purpose is to help people see their own reasons for being, and to remind them that they are temporarily human, and that we are all connected for a short time as humans. My purpose is to lift people up, to help people to see that there are others in and out of this world, who know what is going on in the darkest portions of their lives. My purpose is to provide hope and confirmation that a person may be in pain, but it is temporary. The saying, "This too shall pass," is not cliché, but rather a realistic way of looking at difficult situations. In due time He will strengthen and lift one up. No matter what, no matter who.... Always take care of each other, because that is why we are here.

In the coming chapters you will see how angels play a role in your daily life, and how you can alter the pathway of all those around you, just by being you and being present.

"Do not attempt to be like anyone else, because for all you know, they are trying to be like you." - Dr. Rebecca Foster

CONTRACTS

Who likes contracts? I'm sure no one for that matter, especially because they're binding, and you have to agree to commit to all details listed in them, or you lose. There is one contract we all have, although it is not so much binding, as it is an outline or rudder for decision making; a contract that guides our paths and destination; a contract you signed with your life. Accompanied by this life contract is Free Will, which allows us to make our own decisions, unhampered by Spiritual will. If we have free will, and God has given us the ability to make up our own minds, then why do we have a contract? Is there a destiny? Is our life already figured for us? What is the purpose of a life contract? The answer is that we have a life contract, or outline driven by free will, allowing us to make up our own minds and achieve a destiny that we wanted to obtain long before we were born. Our lives are not figured out for us per say, rather we experience a yearning of our souls to achieve certain character, moral, and spiritual victories.

Well, I call it a life contract, because we write it prior to being born. We sit down with God and determine the best way to learn our life lessons, achieve what we need to achieve, and do it all thankfully in His name. I know, I know, I just made a few heads explode, and some simply shake in disagreement, but seriously, we all have things to do in this life. You may believe or you may not believe there is a higher being, but He is there; you may have simply lost your way of seeing Him. You have the right, and free will, to choose to live as an atheist, a non-believer, an occultist, a cult member, an anti-Christ, or full on Jesus Freak; It is your choice. And although you have the contract, you do not have to follow it. You may regret it in the end, but it is still your choice to do as you please. Free-Will is one of God's greatest gifts. Could you imagine going through life having to do everything your parents told you to do, regardless if it was something you did or didn't want? You would never learn, and you would always hold a grudge. Free will is beautiful. It helps you determine your path, how you end up, and ultimately, who you are in all dealings.

Let us look at this another way so you can see where I am coming from. If you are a parent, you will get this, and if you are not, then maybe someday you will. Everyone wants the best for their children. Most people want their children to grow to become good, upstanding adults who contribute positively to society. Some people want their children to grow a certain way, and some do not care who their children are or become, as long as the child grows up happy. Most parents do not want harm to come to their children; most parents do not want their children in trouble by any means. And most parents forgive their children repeatedly for stupid things they do as they mature. Forgiveness does not stop at painting on the walls or pouring dirt into the toilet. Most parents will stand behind their children regardless of the crimes they commit, the troubles they get into, or the harm they do to themselves and others.

The fact remains that parents love their children unconditionally, most of the time. I say this, because there are cases out there where we might think otherwise, but for the most part, parents forgive their children out of love. When we make our choices, it is the same with our Heavenly Father as with our Earthly parents and our children, we are forgiven, as we forgive. So, before we're born, we sit down with our Heavenly Father to write our contract. We write what we want to learn, such as what it is like to be handicapped, blind, poor, rich, a movie star, a salesmen or woman, a doctor, and so on. We want to learn what it is like to lose a child, lose parents at a young age, learn how to grow; we want to be confident and successful after being raised in a crime infested neighborhood, or learn what it is like to have everything and nothing at the same time.

Imagine the last time you had the opportunity to do something and chose not to, only to regret it later and wish you had chosen otherwise. I do it all the time, thinking of what I should have said at any given moment, but maybe refrained, held back, or said something else. I think…ugh, I should have said this instead and really made my point. We learn everything from the choices we make on a daily basis, both good and bad, positive and negative, success and failure.

Now imagine you have died, and you are shown your last life, the one that just ended. You are sitting there in your 'debriefing' and you see a time in your life when you let someone you loved get away or you took a different path, and you stop and say, "I knew it…I wanted that other way! I wanted that person! I should have chosen differently." To take it another step further, your debriefing is a time of going over what you wanted to learn and what God wanted you to learn. You see where you made mistakes, where you excelled, and where you need work. You relive times that make you aware of desired improvements and you remember your loves, your heart's desires, your happy times and sadness's. You recall 'wanting to do this again' or wondering what it would be like to do this or that. It is a time of going over. We are given a chance to make things up, redo others, and try new experiences. You may decide that you want to know what it is like to meet your spouse earlier in life, or love someone else entirely. Maybe you want to know what it is like to grow up a different race in another country, or maybe just a different neighborhood. You take this time to relax and later decide if coming down is what you want to do again. Considerations are made about who you will spend that time with, how, and what roles they will have in your next life. The debriefing process basically runs you through your last life and helps you to organize your soul goals, regrets, unfulfilled lessons and desires. Take a moment to think of your life now and ponder all the things you have not yet done, do not understand, or wish to experience, and probably some, if not all, of those thoughts will be unattainable in this lifetime for various reasons. Debriefing gives you a lot to think about, and if you feel you finally are the soul you wish to be for eternity.

When you reconsider all you did in your last life, and see all the other lives you lived, then you can make a better educated decision. Good times and bad, loves, losses, chances, opportunities… those are the times that will create the need and want in you to come back and do it again. You may decide to make more choices, new choices, to make better choices and see where you get with those. You may even choose to love differently, more openly, more forgivingly, more compassionately; all of those elements can make a big difference in where a path goes. You may choose your path based on earthly factors such as want, desire, need, hope, disdain, drive, and all the other feelings and reasons that could happen on a human level. But, ultimately, your spiritual self would guide those choices, as well, based off of love, compassion, generosity, patience, and empathy, or the lack of. But again, it is only a guide, a contract, so-to-speak; you simply use it subconsciously to lead the way. Our guides use it, too, and attempt to help us stay the course. This is where listening to your inner voices comes into play.

Listing off all of these important facets of life, do not forget the loved ones. The most important people in your life this time are the most important people in your past lives, they may just be different roles. Passed over loved ones may very well be waiting for you so they can write another life contract including you again. So many facets of our lives are planned, including the people and way we live, but to finally answer the original question, "How you can have a life contract and free will at the same time?" is quite simple. We write what we want to happen, but we forget all of it when we are born. We have our guides,

God, Christ, Allah, Mohammed, Buddha, and other religious figures to whisper in our ears, direct us, and hopefully we listen, hear the message, and act on it, but that is not always the case. We play off much as coincidence or our own thoughts, and second guess choices and decisions. That little voice in the back of our mind is the one we really need to listen to, because although it is faint, it is usually correct. We all have had that moment when we shouted, I KNEW IT, but we changed our minds and figured we were wrong, so we chose B and the answer was A. That is your guides attempting to train you to listen to them. Always go with the first answer. Do not second guess yourself.

Back on track once again. I fall off tracks quite a bit, because I start writing as if I were talking to you in person rather than writing a book, and I just go where my guides take me. If I continue to do that you will be lost, and completely frazzled at what you are reading. So, forgive me for taking you places that I know you may not be ready to go yet. I was writing about life contracts, your life contract to be exact. You are with God, writing your life contract, and you decide who you are going to be, what you want to do, and who you are going to love. You decide how many children you are going to have, or if you are going to learn what it is like to not be able to have children, hence adopt or live without them. You decide the kind of work you will do, maybe as a servant, as I have taken on, or as a healer or communications specialist; regardless of what you choose to do in life, you will always have a reason as to why. The contract is the guide, your free will is the deciding power. You can change all potentials in the blink of an eye, and that is how free will factors into our life contracts.

~~~~~~~~~~~~~~~~~~~~~~~~~~~~~~~

Now, life contracts are funny, because they are always in our subconscious, flitting about, unbeknownst to us until we receive a trigger, or an AH-HA moment, where a light bulb goes off and we are moved. We are unconsciously aware of where we are treading, and we might even feel like something is about to happen, but we just don't know what yet. We know something, though, as we can feel it in our bones. Now I want to explain a hypothetical situation here to deepen your understanding of our contracts and how they affect us. Let us consider Joe this time.

Joe decides that he wants to communicate with God and work for God while he is on Earth. He wants to help reconnect people to Spirit and guide them on their paths. Joe knows this is his job when he is born on Earth; however, Joe's memory of his contract is erased upon birth to prevent him from following a cheat sheet, causing him to work the 'game' on his own, mistakes and all. Let me explain a bit more. If you knew exactly why you were here, who you were supposed to meet, marry, birth, love, and what lessons you were supposed to learn, you would be a full cup your entire life. You would not see any reason in meeting new people, making mistakes, or discovering more possibilities for learning.

A full cup cannot be filled any more. So, in other words, your memory of why you are here is erased so you take your time, learn new things, discover more about yourself, and reach new levels all on your own. If you have ever indulged in a role-play-game such as Zelda for instance, and you did not know anything about the game, you would go more places, explore all regions, meet and talk to people who may or may not help you on your journey, and it would engage you. There are cheats for full Zelda games on the internet, and believe me, it is no fun to cheat. You learn nothing and remember even less. Cheats take you to the boss level before you're ready, and what is the point of even spending the money or time on the game if you're just going to go to the end?

So, Joe does not have cheats; therefore, must play the game of life, one day at a time, step-by-step, wrong and right and forward or backward. The lack of a cheat sheet or even an instruction booklet for that matter, is why Joe does not understand exactly where he is at this point in his life. He may be feeling an inclining towards a coffee shop, harbor, park, or a new relationship, but not fully understand why he all of a sudden is being pulled in any direction. He has entered a new level of growth and is awakening to what is being introduced to him now. Little pushes here and there, signs from loved ones, songs played on the radio, and maybe hearing the name 'Mary' repeatedly over the course of a month, are present in his mind. Eventually it will all make sense as events occur, and things fall into place. This is where you hear people say, "I think this was meant to be."

It may take time to uncover the truth of Joe and Mary meeting, or it may be an instant spark. Just because it is written doesn't mean it will make sense right now. Joe's contract says that he *wants* to meet Mary and fall in love, have four children, buy a house, and live happily ever after. But like I said before, it may not happen based on free will. Choices are ever present. It is also written that Joe will meet Mary while he has a German Shepherd and Mary has a Black cat. In this life, Mary likes boats and will spend a lot of time by the lake watching boats come in and out of a harbor. She will have long brown hair, blue eyes, and a beautiful smile.

Now let's jump ahead to Joe and Mary being born. They grow up and find a career. Joe is working at ABC Communications Company helping people connect to the best deal possible, guiding them to a better bill and cost, and making them happy. He has decided that he wants to go to the park one day and stops to watch the boats come in. He sees a woman sitting on a bench as he strolls along the beachfront. He comments to the woman on the beautiful weather. She comments back about the beauty of the boats on the water. Joe stops. "Hi," he says. "I'm Joe."

She replies, "Hi, I'm Marla." Joe is immediately smitten. Long brown hair, blue eyes, beautiful smile…his type of woman. They fall madly in love, but after a few months they realize it isn't working as something is missing, and they know it will not last.

Joe and Marla break up. He truly thought she was the one and is heartbroken, in addition to being sad at the thought of never meeting the right person. He awakens one day, stretches, and rather than making a cup of joe at home he decides to get a coffee at the local cafe by the lake, and then go for a walk. Joe loves his morning coffee. He orders his coffee and while waiting, he sees a woman sitting at a table playing on her phone. She is beautiful. He moves closer to her while he waits for his order, and as she looks up at him, he says, "Hi, beautiful day today." The woman smiles and says, "Yes, I should be at the lake instead of in here." They laugh, the barista calls Joe's name, and Joe tells Mary to have a nice day before taking his order and leaving.

Two weeks later, Joe decides to go back to the lake to take a walk. He brings his German Shepherd with him this time. As he is walking, he sees that woman from the coffee shop again. He walks by her and says, "Good thing you're enjoying the lake today instead of the coffee shop." She smiles and says, "Hello! Yes, I am taking in the sights and air today! It's beautiful." She then comments on Joe's dog. "Beautiful dog you have, what's his name?" Joe replies, "Gus. He's my buddy, and I'm his human…."

"Joe," Mary interjects, "I remember your name from the coffee shop…. when they called your name. Nice to meet you." Joe is caught off guard as he wonders how and why she remembered his name in only a few moments of meeting each other. Mary is slightly flustered and pauses before she smiles and pets Gus, "I'm Mary. I don't have a dog, but I have a black cat, named Azrael." Mary straightens up and shakes Joe's hand. "Hi. Nice to meet you, Joe." "Likewise," says Joe.

Joe and Mary continue to walk together until Mary says, "I do have to go, I have a meeting this afternoon," as she grabs her car keys. Joe spots a big blue boat dangling on her keychain. "Do you like boats?"

"Yes," Mary replies, "they are my passion; although I don't ever get out on any, I do love watching them." Mary realizes something has clicked. Joe is wondering what just happened, as he feels a connection that he does not understand. The harmony of their life paths just collided, and they are both very aware of the energy created in that moment. Joe gets Mary's number before she leaves, and the rest is history.

Now to understand this scenario better, you must understand a few more things. We all have a type of person we 'go' for. This is partially caused by our previous life loves, races, customs, etc. (mind blown), as well as what we are looking for in a person this time around. For instance, I have always liked dark hair, dark skin, and a wide back and shoulders; obviously, this is due to residual energy from a previous life. It is the type of guy I have always gone for; however, my husband is slightly different. Taking a few steps back to indulge you, I once had a reading from a friend who read playing cards. She said that I would meet, or had already met, a man different from any man I had ever dated, and we would be married. I thought of everyone I knew and could not think of anyone I would consider marrying out of the lot. No way. Let me go back a bit further. Every guy I had dated and who had broken my heart was a 'J' name. I vowed to never date anyone again with a "J" in his name. I believed I had, and still believe, I have the residual want and desire for a Scottish Highlander left in my memory, whom I deeply loved. (At least that is what I picture.)

I contemplated that reading for a long time, and I never let anyone read me, ever, but she was a friend who I worked with and we were bored, so I let her have some fun with me. Truly, I never let anyone read me again, except for a bible reading many years later. If you're wondering what a bible reading is, basically an old woman read me out of the bible. She pulled verses and parables that tied to me and my current situations. She told me where I was going wrong with my gift, and how I needed to correct it using the bible. It was my second awakening in regard to how I read people and opened me up to simply hearing and seeing information rather than using tarot cards or other forms of divination. It was God saying..." USE ME!!!!!!" That is a bible reading.

Now to go back even further. I had met a friend of my brother's; he was in a relationship that was on its last leg, and I was in a semi-serious relationship, as well. I first looked at him and thought, nope, not my type, but a nice guy. I actually ended one relationship, entered a 'bridge' relationship that helped me get out of a toxic relationship, and when it didn't last, entered a relationship I thought was fated and destiny, all before I started dating my husband. I have always just followed my heart.

Holy cows, what on earth do I mean? Well…I took advantage of a relationship that helped me gain back my confidence to leave an unhealthy relationship. It worked, and it didn't last, and I was okay with that. I then met someone whom I thought it was fated-to-be due to all the little things that fell into place. He was different than anyone I had ever dated, as well. However, I realized that he was saying and doing things in our relationship that I had experienced before. I was saddened by this, and I knew that my guides were putting me through a lesson. Does Rebecca need to learn this again, or has she figured it out yet? I knew I did not have to learn what it was like to date an alcoholic again or live with addiction in my partner. I cried. I decided, and I ended the relationship.

I was now free to be me, to fill in any negative voids that had appeared, and then work to get back on my path as a complete soul and person. I knew I was off, and that I had to focus and pull my energy in. I spent time with my older brother on weekends doing Karaoke, and sometimes his friend, Brian, would come along. I went out by myself and enjoyed the time I had getting to know me and who I wanted to be. I found myself playing around with Brian, messing with him, flirting with him, but at the same time keeping my distance. We spent several months just hanging out, all of us, having fun, and I enjoyed the time I spent with my brother, too. Reverting back to above, when we met, we were both in relationships; however, our relationships with others fizzled out, and we soon found ourselves looking at one another differently. Like I said, I did not know anyone whom I would consider dating, and I waited to see if my friend's reading for me would ever come true. I was doubtful.

Weekends were fun and I got all the karaoke in that my little heart wanted. My brother, Brian and I would simply hang out and just have a good time. All was fine until Brian obtained a job out of town, and he had to move away. I found myself wondering about him, realizing I was going to miss him. He was in and out of a situation with a woman who was living in another state, so I didn't want to mess with that, yet I didn't want him to leave without letting him know how I felt. Basically, we were single, but emotions are complicated. I asked him, "So what are you going to do in Dixon, Illinois? You're not married. You have no kids, what are you going to do, tip cows? You're going to miss me too much." Yes, I was fishing.

I said, "Aren't you going to get married? What about kids? You're going to be a lonely boy." He replied, "I am never getting married again (He was married and divorced twice before), and I am *never* having children." I was disappointed. I had a son from a previous marriage, and he was my life when it came to decisions, so I had to make one more attempt. I said, "So when are you going to show me your new place?" He answered, "Tomorrow. You can come home with me and we'll go shopping. I need new work shirts." It all fell into place after that. He ended his long-distance relationship for good, and from that date, August 28th we dated three months and were married November 21st.

Brian was like no person I had ever dated before. His hair was lighter than the others, and his skin was lighter, as well. He did, however, have a wide back, stood 6'4" tall, and was strong enough in my eyes to toss a few cabers. The closest I have come to seeing him toss cabers, though, is when he throws 14-foot 4x4s across the lawn to build a playhouse. How does all of this fit into this chapter on contracts and destinies? Let me get down to the nitty-gritty here. The first guy I ever kissed was a Brian in 8th grade. I left a relationship once for a Brian, and Brian's middle name is Jay. Go figure! I was looking for a "J" name the whole time (although I vowed to never date one again), and I subconsciously knew I was looking for a Brian but did not put 2-and-2 together until it happened. Looking back is so cool, so pay attention now to your history and what attracts you. What's even funnier is that his first wife was Lynn and his second wife's middle name was Lynn...and he commented that he had better be careful with another Lynn.

I knew someone else, let's call him Christian, who dated a Jacque. She was pregnant at the time, not with his child, and she ended up becoming more of his family member than his girlfriend. Christian and Jacque broke up but remained friends. Later, Christian dated and got engaged to an Angelica. They were together quite a while, but things didn't work out between them. Fast forward ten years and Christian met and married a Jacque. They had two children together. However, Christian met a woman named Angelica. He could not avoid the draw to Angelica, as this was the way his path was to take him. Christian and Jacque divorced, and he married Angelica. This is a hard lesson to figure, but when you look at the entire spiritual contract, you can see that as hard as it was to follow that path, he listened to his heart, and knew what he was meant to do.

And, my brother Andy. I cannot leave him out. He dated three Karen's at the same time. Yes, three women named Karen, all of whom he juggled at once. He later met and married Kara; his partner in crime, and equal on all levels. They truly complement one another. When I asked him if he had any other 'moments' of recollection where his past happened too soon and caught up with him later, he could not recall. Nothing else made sense to him. My younger brother Matt does not have any past/future similarities that I can recall. He did have a thing with women whose names started with an "M", but other than that I cannot think of any that drew him to something or someone.

I have several stories of exes who found true love after me too. One ex told me that he had met the girl of his dreams, she was just like me without all the baggage. He married her shortly after we broke up. Another ex-boyfriend started dating and finally married the love of his life, and we actually look like sisters. I love her, too, as she is an amazing soul, and they are both more like family to me now. I was simply the mistaken one they both thought they were supposed to be with; however, I was not the one, just similar... a resemblance of who their souls were looking for this lifetime. And I can guarantee that you've heard at least once in your life, "Oh my gosh! Did you see so-n-so? He's dating someone now and she looks just like Blank!" Neither a coincidence, nor a hankering for that last person, but to put it simply, their soul knows who they are looking for, and they made a mistake initially. Those are a part of our contracts. Similarities in partners basically means that someone knows what and who they are looking for in a partner, they just aren't sure which one.

Let me go back to Joe, whom I was chattering about earlier. His career choice was to come down and help God, rather he came down and started working for ABC Communications Company. He knew that he was supposed to communicate with people, help them, and guide them, console them, and lead them in a helpful direction, but instead, he misunderstood which kind of communications. Someone like Joe only needs clarification and confirmation of what he sees, feels, hears, and goes through daily to wake him up to his real purpose here on Earth. Sometimes people figure this out on their own, yet sometimes people are directed to or find someone like me in the process. It becomes very clear to me from the get-go that I am reading for someone who needs direction to do what they promised to do when they came down here.

This is a very rewarding experience for me, because I get to see what a person is going through, what they have perceived, and what they are missing in terms of spiritual and Godly interventions. Helping people to see the correlations between what they are doing currently in life, what they have done, and who and what they are supposed to be is one of the most significant reasons I continue reading. An awakening is happening. An awakening means that someone is about to shed all their Earthly ideas and open themselves up to their spiritual counterpart. It is lovely.

Some people are open to the idea of awakening and learning more about themselves, but what about the people who think this is a bunch of bushwa or do not believe in God or Spiritual intervention? What if they believe this is all it is and then we die and go into darkness? All I can say is that there are people out there who truly believe in all of those things. I have met them, and I know them. To some, the truth is shut out due to anger at God. It is usually anger over a loss or a pain they suffered; it may also be anger over the bad things that happen in our human worlds daily like war, poverty, abuse, death, murder, addiction,

kidnapping, hate - and the list goes on. But I revert to how I started this chapter; we have free will.

People come into this life and live by making choice after choice. Some choose good, and some choose otherwise. Some listen to the dark angels as they yell in their ears to do something, rather than listen for the angel's whispers in an attempt to direct them correctly. This is a choice everyone makes. People ask me, "Was my son supposed to die? Whose fault is it?" It depends on if that was a life choice, or a contractual end. It may be the choice of a person to die a certain way, such as cancer or illness; however, the choice of a person to get behind the wheel while drunk is a poor free will choice and probably wasn't written into either life contract. This gets complex though, because a person may have it written to suffer from an accident and pull through it in order to learn perseverance and determination. Both would learn here, and I don't want to confuse you. There is choice and purpose to everything. Again, choices are made by others' free will that affect everyone's lives. This is a tough subject. Yes, some people come into the world with a set date of death for a various reason, but if someone is killed or murdered, it is the choice of the other person to do this act. Free will, beliefs, faith...they all play a role in a person's actions.

So, is there a hell? Yes. There is a hell, and I have seen it. I once did a gallery at a friend's house. She held the party in her living room and situated the seating U-shaped in front of a fireplace. I stood facing the fireplace with the women on either side of me. In the front of the fireplace to my right, a man jumped out of a fiery blaze and he was gnashing his teeth and reaching for me. I explained his situation and he did not move from that spot but continued to growl and flail. The woman I was reading for explained that this was her stepfather and he had murdered her mother. It was an amazing confirmation for her that he was in hell for his actions. I can tell you, though, that not all murderers go to hell. Mercy is given when a person truly sees the error of their way and understands that an act was heinous or egregious; however, they must repent and ask for forgiveness with all their being for this to be true.

Like I said earlier...a parent will forgive their child of the most awful acts, and this is one of them. Hard to believe, I get it might be for some, but for those who believe in God's sovereign ability to love and forgive, then you will see this is truly possible. That does not mean the person will ever be able to forgive themselves, though. Forgiving ourselves is one of the hardest things we can ever do aside from forgiving others. The problem is that self-forgiveness resides in our heart, and we can say it all we want, but if we don't *accept* it into our bones, and *wholly* believe it, then it is untrue. I do go into this further in other chapters, because self-forgiveness is what we need in order to move through to the light, otherwise we judge ourselves unworthy and end up in a darker place...but that is another story.

Remember that contracts are outlines and frameworks of how our lives should be lived, they are not blueprints. They are not exact measurements of goals, lessons, and distances traveled. Contracts neither denote what the end will be, nor do they provide us with an explanation of how to handle issues. The lessons we are here to learn and the steps we take along the way all help us achieve a higher spiritual level. We are here to grow and become better souls, better people, and energies that heal rather than tear apart. We are supposed to love one another above all else, because love overcomes a multitude of sins. And if you're wondering, yes, this verse is from 1 Peter 4:8, and is one of my most favorite chapters in the Bible, because it saved me when no one knew I was suffering and at my end. If you are ever going to preach the bible, make sure you are loving someone above all else, not judging them or stuffing religion down their throat...make sure you love them first.

AWAKENING YOUR SPIRITUAL GIFT

"An awakening is discovering reality and grasping the knowledge that there's more to this life in this world than just the Earthly things; for some, that Awakening comes when the rugs have been ripped out from underneath their feet. It's when a person is spiritually, emotionally, and sometimes physically being dragged across the rocks on the bottom, and they realize that they do not have the strength on their own to get through it. Awakening is when someone finally reaches up to something they can't see, in blind faith, and strength will be given to them. This is when they are ready to accept their abilities."

– Dr. Rebecca Foster

Awakening happens when you are at your end, your worst, your lowest. A lot of people ask me how I got started doing readings. My experience wasn't so much a beautiful awakening where I was sitting in a lotus blossom and it opened, and fairies brought me dew drops to freshen up. It was ghastly and powerful at the same time. I was young, I was angry, and I did not love myself or anyone around me, including God, Christ, and the Holy Spirit. I rejected everyone, and I did not want to live anymore. I felt nothing around me but darkness, and I was sinking into a pit of hell. I was depressed, sad, and full of hate. I had no idea what to do, and no one knew what I was going through. I was 13 years old, and I was seeing demons, hearing voices, and was aware that there were more than the eyes could see everywhere; no one knew. I was alone. I was bad. I was a misfit.

I was such a difficult child, so lost, and so terribly hateful to everyone, and the only thing my parents thought to do was have me visit with a psychiatrist. I was enveloped in a darkness, and I was pushing all the light away emotionally, verbally, and spiritually. I even had the psychiatrist convinced that I was completely crazy; in reality, I was (unknowingly to others) quite good at reading people, so I knew how to behave, and how to become who they thought I was, or should be. I convinced the psych that I was crazy, and then I had to convince him I wasn't, all by taking a 500-question test. Do you see ghosts? Do you believe in demons? Do you talk to dead people? The first time I answered yes, yes, and yes, and the second time I answered no, no and no. It was all a joke to me, because I knew I wasn't completely crazy, but I did know that I was seeing all of those things that were mentioned in the test, so I had to figure out what was going on.

To tell you the truth, I was willing to be consumed by darkness, namely the Devil, or Satan, or Beelzebub, or whatever name you want to call him. I had shunned God and yelled to Him that I did not love Him. I yelled to Him that I hated Him, and that He had let me down. I told Him I never wanted Him in my life again, and I put all my trust in the Devil. I was a very defiant and unruly child, and I was angry. I was angry that my parents divorced, I was angry that my father was such a drunken jerk, and I was angry at my mother for being…my mother. I cannot explain it in any simpler terms. Most of all, I hated me, and I wanted to die.

~~~~~~

My oldest brother was also living a life of turmoil, and he was quite lost; to be honest, I think he is surprised to this day that he is still alive. I looked up to and admired him greatly; I, also, admired his ability to live in turmoil and *survive*. I smoked, I drank, and I ran around. I was young and stupid, and I listened to no one. I did not care if I lived or died, and I did not care if anyone cared either. My desire to reach out to the darker side of things was real, because it was a true manifestation of my defiance. My brother was connected to the darker side of things, and he could make some scary things happen. I was not around to witness most of it, but stories have been told that scared even the most unshakeable of his friends; I was impressionable.

To make a long story short, I opened myself up to the dark side and I didn't care. One experience that still causes me to tremble happened in my bedroom. I had a large dollhouse, that my father had put a lot of sweat into building, which sat on my floor in front of my bedroom window. I created a séance room in the attic with a table, chairs, and an Ouija board with a pallet on the table. I created little books with pentagrams on them and stacked them haphazardly around the room. In addition to my little ghost room, I had created several of my own Ouija boards and I hung them on my wall. These little trinkets were not just drawings or figures, rather horcruxes that I put my life and energy into, almost as my own protection from being damaged and hurt. They truly carried their own energies. I continued to turn away from the Lord. I put my heart and energy into the boards and doll house. I was still too young to understand the effect it was having on me, or my soul.

I will say it now and preach this forever - you should not *use* an Ouija Board. I say use, because most people jump on a board without question, or protection, and "play" with it. Playing with any kind of tool improperly will open the door to things you don't want to happen. The energies from an Ouija board want to tap into a life; when your guard is down, hopefulness is up, and you're willing to accept anything that comes through for the fun of it, then you can expect negative outcomes, as well as unwanted attachments.

The energies that come through are tricksters and are dark, and *under no circumstances,* should people use them alone; loneliness opens a heart even more. In addition, if you think you're talking to your grandma, you're not; let me give you an example. My grandmother lived in a house that her family built in 1911 and is one of the oldest houses in the village of Palos Park, Illinois. Everyone who lived in this house, died in this house, with the exceptions of my grandfather, who was in the hospital at his time of death, and my grandmother who passed in a nursing home.

At the time my grandmother passed away, she was the last in her family to die. My brother, his previous wife, and their children, shared the home with my grandmother, and cared for the home while she was in the nursing home. They eventually stayed, even after she passed, and continued to fix up the house. My sister-in-law, at the time, decided to whip out an Ouija Board, by herself, and began to use it in the kitchen. She later came to me and said, "Oh, I'm talking to grandma." I asked, "On what?" She said, "The Ouija board." I was like, "Ummm…no you are not. My grandma is in heaven, and she wouldn't talk to you anyway, especially on a board. Don't kid yourself." She was not talking to my grandma, rather something telling her that it was my grandma. There were lots of things in that home all my life, and several of us experienced them firsthand on the Ouija board. Nothing good comes from them, and I am sure I have an attachment to this day because of my Ouija Board usage. Again, don't use forms of divination for play; they open people up to energies that they do not want opened. This becomes especially true when ignorance is mingled with a tool. Ouija boards are fun, but you should not *play* with one, as they are not toys, but rather tools; tools in the wrong hands can do big damage.

I have found many times that it takes feeling the emptiness of darkness to realize that you not only seek but want the light. This was me! I realized I had opened doorways that were bound to get me in trouble. I realized that darkness was real, and that it was the part of the dimensions that are void of light. I did not want to be in darkness; I wanted to see. I knew that I could see, hear, and talk to 'things,' but I did not yet understand the extent. I felt lost and terrified that I had pushed my Heavenly Father away, and full-on believed I was going to hell. I was 13 years old standing in my blue bedroom, and I dropped to my knees on my green shag carpet. I put my hands together and clenched my fingers tightly. I raised my arms and my chin, and I cried. I begged God to take me back.

I begged Him to forgive me for all the hateful things I had said and done. I begged Him to not send me to hell, rather I would be His servant for the rest of my life, and I would work for Him - *only* for Him. I cried hard that night. No one knew of my suffering, my wanting to just die, my hope for a new beginning... except God, and of course, the dog, because I told her everything.

I truly repented, not only out of fear of what I had done, but also because I knew what I was experiencing was not of this Earth. I knew there was something else out there in that darkness, so something *had* to be out there in the light. I did not change overnight, or become an angel in the same time, but I was on my way to attempting to understand my relationship with God and my purpose here.

I began to see 11:11 everywhere; I did not understand it at the time, but *it was everywhere*. I continued to work on my relationship with God, and with Christ, because I knew them, just not intimately at that point. Here, I want to add that who you pray to, is all that matters; your relationship with the Heavenly Being is all that matters. A major misconception is that you must go to church to believe in God or know

God, but this is wrong. A relationship with God is personal and intimate. A relationship with the church depends on how invested you are with their goings-on. Attending church opens you up to a possible fellowship with its members, but it may neither be for you, nor the right avenue to get you to what you seek. God will call you to be where you are supposed to be, when you are supposed to be there. I go to church when He says, "Rebecca, there is a message for you at church today."

Seeing 11:11, feeling the great desire to know Spirit, or feeling the desperate need to reconcile your soul may not be how it is for everyone, due to our different paths. Some may wake up sooner than others, and some may never wake up at all. The point is that you must be aware of your own path and goings-on, your own tribulations and issues, the mountains you have to climb, and the rivers you are to cross. You must be aware of how you handle the issues, as well as how you perceive those troubles, either as temporary, as a punishment, or maybe even as a lesson. It is fun when I read for people who are not seeing the signs, and then suddenly, just because it is pointed out, they know what to look for; their world opens up to Spirit, Guides, and God's work in their lives. It is momentous; spiritual presence is now recognized. It's the same concept as when you buy a certain car and then suddenly you see your car everywhere, or you become conscious of a name and then every other person you meet shares that name. I love when life aligns with mission, consciousness, and purpose. Most excellent!!

Many times, I have been asked how you will know if you are supposed to wake up or are being called to do God's work. I mentioned 11:11, earlier, as well as some other numbers that play constant roles in our daily lives. Now, what exactly is 11:11, you ask? It is an alarm clock…an awakening that says, "You promised to do certain things when you went down there, and now you must start doing them!" It is your guides trying to wake you up with repeated visuals and feelings that enable you to reach your fullest potential, your Reason, your purpose. Wake up!

An awakening is not easy for everyone, and I speak from personal experience. Some people are reluctant to learn more about it, maybe out of fear of the unknown, or simply the fear of not living up to expectation. Some are afraid of going against what they have been raised to believe about relationships with God, and some take all of this a step further and call it the devil's work. I don't see how saving people and introducing them to God, Spirit, the Bible, Christ, and living a purposeful life is the devil's work, but we will let them have that one. As humans, we can only do so much, and we must leave the rest to God; He is really more convincing, believe me.

Not having walked in someone's shoes makes discerning their apprehension to discover their spirituality more difficult. Some may have a relationship to repair with God, as did I, while some may not yet even know Him. Some may have been raised to ignore, or not believe in anything but what a church teaches. But, believe me…. there is more to your relationship with God than what the bible teaches! It is intimate. It is fun. It is laughter. It is between you and Him. All things are possible; the gravity of seeing what I have been taught without knowing it in the bible is tremendous! Being directed to certain authors and chapters, or verses without prior knowledge of that exact verse is amazing. I laugh and cry and cheer and praise…. because recognizing and opening up to your spiritual self is an amazing journey that deserves praise.

An awakening may be happening to you right now. You may be looking around and touching your chin, mouth open saying, "…. I get this…." Yet again, you might be the person who does not recognize signs, meaning you are too focused on the Earthly things happening around you to notice them. I can almost guarantee after reading this book that you will hear and see things differently, as your energy is reconnected to your heavenly home and truths.

An example of purpose lost on Earthly matters is represented in a young man I had read for, who was reluctant to open to his gift; he was being tortured mentally by the darker things that knew why he was here. Meaning, he was unaware that he was to be doing God's work, but the darker things were fully aware and were attempting to shut him down. He could hear voices that he misjudged as his own, and there was an entity, or elemental, that was messing with his head. I tried to help him understand that he was listening to the wrong voices, but he shut down and ignored me. As much as I wanted to help him and others, I can only do so much. Everyone must realize when to release someone or something, because sometimes hanging on, hurts more than letting go. You can only be you and live to do your best. It is so difficult, I know, and I am no hypocrite, so I will be the first to admit that letting go of the people we love, or believe we should love, is one of the hardest things to do. I, too, have wrestled with this, and still do, even today.

I apologize because I find it so hard to stay focused while I am writing. I see so much, and things just pop into my head and I don't want to miss anything to tell you!!! We were talking about numbers! It is funny how many people can recognize signs after I point them out, such as pennies, feathers, and dimes out of nowhere; another common sign often recognized is 11:11, or triple digits regularly displayed around them. Once people realize that all those little things they have been seeing *actually mean something*, they are able to awaken to their messages and finally start to listen. Regardless of my impact on a person, the little signs, songs, and miracles will cause an awakening person to pause and wonder if their question was just answered, or if a response was given to act, or sit calmly by and wait. Believe me - the more you listen, the more messages and guidance you will receive, and the more attuned you will become to God, Spirit, and your path.

Gosh, I hope that those who do not believe, or ignore, or shut out, take a second glance when they start to see and recognize the signs they are receiving to wake up, and that they are able to at least acknowledge that their guides are with them. I hope if you are one of those people right now saying, *"Garbage!"* that a blessing will come your way in the form of a penny, or a feather, or a dime to say…. "Hi, we're here with you!"

Of course, there are people who are aware of the signs and messages, but do not know how to fully open up to, and/or understand them. I enjoy helping people understand their connection to Spirit and help them to see that even though they are here on earth, they still maintain that silver thread connection. For some this is a breakthrough, to finally realizing they are not just seeing or hearing things and are not crazy, rather, they are experiencing a supernatural event in their life that they had forgotten at birth. When I am on the phone, there is a point when I can hear the 'A-Ha' moment, telling me a person has understood the messages coming through. When in person I can see that moment as a glint in their eyes or the way they hold their breath. I know when a person is 'reached.'. I can also see when someone is blocking messages and does not want to accept what is being passed on to them, maybe because they have a reputation to uphold with others as being relentlessly hardheaded, they simply don't believe, or they are scared.

Either way, it is exciting to know that their lives are forever changed, because now, all those little moments that may have gone by as coincidence, or left misunderstood, have proved to hold meaning. People realize how God is at work in their lives, and how their lives have meaning and purpose. For some, this realization is what they needed to overcome a hurdle, or to see that they are not just here to waste time. People finally can make sense of events, issues, and challenges, and are able to see that what they have been doing all along has made a difference, not only in their own lives, but the lives of others, as well. This is the information that I see, share, and confirm for people; *this is my Why.*

An awakening, for some, may mean that they are no longer looking at the ground, consumed with how much money they make, or what kind of car they drive. So much of the time, we are worried about what we have or can provide; yet, we forget that being rich does not pertain to your bank account. An awakening may mean that a person is physically depleted and no longer has the strength to go on. The physical aspect of living is all they have depended on up to this point and have considered to be their life source; but, hopefully, they realize there is more strength out there at their disposal. This does not always happen, although when it does, they may shout, "Hey! I got through something amazing and I don't know how, or maybe I am just that awesome!" Not knowing Spirit is a difficult existence, one that I could not imagine, simply because I know I am nothing without God, and Christ, and I know I cannot succeed without them. I do not attempt anything without discussing it with Him first, and when I take my first, second and third steps, I listen for that, *'Stop,'* feeling, or, *'Turn around!'* gut instinct; I trust it all implicitly. Maybe this is what needs to be discovered by all people, and maybe if more people listened and watched for these signs and feelings, the world would be a more considerate place.

When we awaken, we are starting from the bottom. We are usually at the lowest of lows, and there is nowhere to go but up or out. This is the place where we are lifted and strengthened; this is also a place where we bow our heads in thankfulness. It is called humility.

Humility is a part of awakening, because you finally see how small you are in the world, yet how much of an impact you can really have - it is truly invigorating and inspiring! Nothing can take away the passion that develops from an awakening. What was once empty can now be filled; and God takes full advantage of filling you with His love, acceptance, forgiveness, and passion. It is that passion, and knowledge that nothing happens without intervention of some kind, along with a full acceptance of giving oneself over to Spirit, and the removal of ego, which can only be one thing; *it is a rebirth.*

I do not take credit for anything. I give it all to God. If I read someone and they are amazed, I give it to God. If I invent something, I give it to God. We have the capacity within our brains to compute, consider, and logically understand; however, our minds are where the

inspiration to create, invent, discover, and see beyond what is in front of us comes from, and is also where God speaks to us.

Oh, the fun we will have in later chapters.......and, I must say, that it is very difficult not to just jump into another train and take off; I am struggling right now to stay on track. Better yet...I will stop here and go there.

INCARNATE ANGELS & OLD SOULS

Incarnate angels are awakening more and more. What are incarnate angels and why are they here? Incarnate angels are people who once lived as angels but *chose* to give up that existence to come down and live as humans. They are the people whom everyone goes to with their problems and usually they struggle with their weight most of their lives. What?! Why? These souls, unknowing of their positions and purposes on earth, tend to wrestle with balancing all of the troubles that come their way and they also pack on the pounds during stressful times, or all their lives, in an attempt to protect themselves from others' negative energy. Not only do these people have to deal with their own issues, they attract people with problems as well. The trouble is that they don't know how to say No, and they find themselves drowning in guilt and sadness due to others' failures and their inability to help the troubled.

Oh, there is so much to share here.

These people will usually find themselves surrounded by those needing healing, help, guidance, love, direction, and handholding. It could encompass those in the health industry, mainly nurses and physicians, who are open to natural or spiritual healings in addition to their traditional medical training. I must include hairdressers and bar tenders, because they see and hear their share of carnage in a day's work, and strangers tend to spill their guts while in their company. Not only do hairdressers and bar tenders observe and provide guidance, but they also carry others at times, working as vessels of wisdom for the troubled souls who sit in their chairs. Servants of God come in many forms.

Incarnate angels may find themselves surrounded by family and friends who are addicted, abused, or manipulated in life. It is not anyone's place to change another individual as this is solely the will of each person and they must realize the need and make the moves to change on their own. Incarnate angels need to know when to walk away from a problem or a troubled person, because even Jesus knew when to walk away and rest; even He knew when it was time to turn away and let things be as they were. Sometimes holding on hurts more than letting go. Remember that.

Incarnate angels will spend a lifetime helping others, giving up for themselves, and making concessions. They will fight to help others stand when those individuals don't want to stand on their own. They will go wherever they are needed, and sometimes not even know where that is. They may never set out for just one path in life; instead, they live in the moment, unaware that their presence has meaning and purpose, healing, and saving grace. Is this you? Are you surrounded by people who seem to always need help, handholding, and guidance? Are you always attempting to save someone? I may be writing about you. Have you given up on people? Does humanity frustrate and anger you? I may be writing about you, too. How is that possible? Let me explain. When you come down here to work for God, no matter the capacity, you begin with the understanding that you have maybe 100 years to accomplish your goals. By the time you reach an age to follow that instinct, you are probably in your late teens. Enter life, family, work, earthly paths, and education, family expectations, personal desires, and self-discovery…a plate full of choices and decisions, chaos galore. We are finally, hopefully, free to choose whom we want to be and where we want to go, although sometimes not. While we are deciding all these earthly choices, our souls start to shine, directing us in another way.

Suddenly, out of nowhere, the desire to be a high-profile doctor turns into a Doctors-without-Borders desire…or street musician, or freelance artist. No one understands this desire in you, you weren't raised that way, and you are now in turmoil about making people, and

This vision was of a man who had left his comfort zone for the unknown. The bridge represented the need to leave one part of life he had outgrown, for a destination he had never experienced before. He was met with an overgrown forest and hedge. He was provided with a machete to cut his way through, his own way through, this dense new beginning of possibilities. Although choices were his, he was still guided by Spirit and inspired as to which directions to take. Scary decisions and choices may be terrifying, but there are times we already know what is right or wrong and the decision to get up and start the journey is up to us. He could have turned down this opportunity and simply wallowed in his misery, but he didn't.

yourself, happy (enter bridges, boulders, and rivers, which you will read about in several places and contexts throughout the book).

Okay, so, the realization hits that you only have 100 years on earth, and you start to awaken to the fact that humans are in trouble. We are the fighting, hating, judging, hurting, conflicting, and close-minded people of the world; no one wants to see the other person's perspective or view, and everyone wants to convince others of their own beliefs, or they decide they can no longer be friends. Forget the fact that in previous lives, someone who is currently White was once Black, and probably lived as a slave at one point, and Blacks were once White and lived as slave owners in a different time. We are here to learn about different perspectives, views, experiences, and troubles. People tend to only live in the moment, with little consideration for the bigger picture. Seeing this daily struggle, minute-by-minute, with all people, is truly heartbreaking. The feelings come across as contempt and disdain for people in general, due to the subconscious need to make great Earthly changes; however, the question always arises as to how one person can do it all themselves. This is the struggle of an incarnate angel. I'm just lil ol' me…what can I do? Be humble. Understand you are a soul here to learn too. Growing to be more Christlike… (Holy cows she did not just write that!!) Yes, I did…and you can fill that in any way you want, but for me…. I call my Savior Christ.

Now, imagine the weight of the world is on your shoulders, and you cannot yet fully understand or even comprehend your part in all the universal goings-on. You *are* just a human after all, right? Enter the stress of attempting to save the world. As I mentioned before, incarnate angels tend to struggle with weight throughout their lives, losing and gaining repeatedly. This is due to the subconscious attempt to protect oneself from negative energies, both human, and otherwise. Instead of embracing the light and surrounding the body in a white glow of heavenly protection, incarnate angels eat. Have you ever heard someone say that they are a stress eater? If you're a stress eater, after considering all you are dealing with, you may want to examine things a little closer and discern if the problems are your own, or someone else's, then decide then and there to let go of what you can and adorn yourself in a cloak of white light.

Most incarnate angels deal with other people's issues in an attempt to keep that person afloat. The stress they deal with is usually brought on by self or energy attraction, and they liken the need for protection by packing on the weight through eating (Your vibe attracts your tribe). Once an incarnate angel recognizes that they eat when stressed out, they may want to practice protective lights, or meditations before they head to the cupboard looking for their relief.

I have met many incarnate angels in my lifetime, and when they realize who and what they are in connection to this life, it is as if the weight of sadness, depression, hardships - you name the difficulty - is lifted off their shoulders. They realize they have a purpose, that all of the negativities in their lives have not been in vain, and in fact, *do* have meaning. Not all people who are here to help are incarnate angels, though; some just come down to help because they have numerous lives behind them, which have amounted to remarkable experiences, thus, becoming what we call 'old souls.'

An incarnate angel is different from an old soul, though, because an old soul may not want to come down again. I am one of those souls. I did not want to come back down, and I fought it by not taking my first breaths. Doctors had to stick my feet with pins to get me to breathe, and all at once, I came into this world like a sonic boom. My son Benjamin is just like me in that way. He is my 90-year-old soul, pissed off that he had to come back down, angry that he had to be a child again and annoyed by having to be told what to do. I am sure he was a General in some war, who died a happy, grumpy, stubborn old man, and then got the news that he had to come back down. He has been screaming and upset since the day he was born; it makes us laugh, but I get him.

Old souls are aged, possibly immature, and not angelic…you may know one or two. They carry defiance and discord with authority and tend to strive to be the authority, coupled with high intelligence and a silver tongue. We actually joke that my Benjamin is so amazing that he will either be President of Mars or the next Super Villain, but regardless, he will do amazing things. It is funny to start seeing these different people in your life, because you will then start to see a beautiful design, impeccable and divinely created to ensure spiritual growth and love. Take a look at your family and friends and discern each person…. why are you all together and how do you relate?

I want to differentiate between incarnate angels and old souls further because they are two different beings, with different histories and experiences; both are here to change the world for the better, yet they do so in very different ways.

Incarnate angels find it easy to do the right things, as this is their nature, whereas, given the same situation, old souls may choose to quietly 'sit this one out' because they just don't want to be there or anywhere, or around people. Old souls may even be very social, yet hermit-typed and appear anti-social at the same time. This comes down to their disdain for people and ignorance. They know we only have a bit of time here and are frustrated by the lack of movement towards Worldly betterment by society as a whole. They are likable and charismatic but hate the world for its stupidity and lack of compassion for one another. There is contempt for people who are ignorant of others. Both incarnate angels and old souls share that quality, and while angels become sad and frustrated at the possibility of not making a change, old souls become angry, frustrated, and probably swear a lot, because deep down they know they only have about 100 years to make a difference. Incarnate angels get caught up in others' drama because they want to fix everything; old souls will help others to an extent but can cut ties faster than a person jumping out of bed at the sound of a cat hacking up a hairball. There is only so much one person can do, and recognizing your purpose in another's life is essential, so you do not want to waste time and energy.

Regardless of the age of your soul, or your current awareness situation, you are supposed to be here. It may be to only make the world function on a financial level, or ensure that work gets done, but remember that anyone can wake up at any time. How someone handles that wake-up call is up to them. Some wonder what the heck is going on, while others recognize the signs and open up immediately. Some see that the earthly stuff is all just stuff and they want more out of life, people, relationships, jobs, careers, etc., than what we have been living with, which usually causes the strife. When you wake up, your eyes are opened, and you hear what is going on around you. You start to listen to direction, following the signs placed in front of you. When this happens, you are then more aware of the darker angels around you, as well as how they press and push to bring you down, defeat you, and make you feel lost, crazy, or insignificant. Darker angels will also use others to do their bidding, and if others are willing to listen to them, it can wreak havoc in once-loving relationships. Once you have arrived here, you realize it is time to change your course and trample on. *Do not* give in or call it quits, as this is the point of awakening! You may fall down a time or two, but hopefully, you find the strength to climb upwards.

We all have a destiny, a purpose, and reason; some are aware of that reality, and some just go through life as if it is happening around them. There is a blessing to awareness, yet it is difficult as well because now you see what needs to be done, like a director behind the curtains…you are not just in attendance at the show, now you are

producing it. Imagine that awareness and stress…I know some of you are

right now. Regardless if you are an incarnate angel or an old soul, or

maybe you're just here to figure things out, know that you are never

alone and the hierarchy of energies around you, both visible or not, are

always there to help and guide you. Realize that you have a lot of

purpose here, and some may take the servant's role, both as a career and

a spiritual path, while some may simply live their lives, it doesn't matter.

What matters is that we consider each person and that their lives are

probably not simple and give each other a bit of a break. Easier said than

done sometimes, because I'd like to share my mind with some people

and that will probably never change.

Earlier I wrote that I am an old soul, and I also wrote that I did

not want to be here. I have to say that I love this life, and I love being

here. I don't want to leave for that matter. I immensely enjoy this life,

my family and friends, the lessons I have learned, the pains I have

experienced, the joys that have lifted me up, and the path that I have

walked. I would not change a thing, because each moment, both good

and bad has made me exactly who I am as I sit here writing this book.

My regrets, directions, ups and downs, loves, losses, hates, words, thoughts, and walks have all led me here, and I would not change a moment, unless we count stepping on Legos in the dark. The point is that, even though I may have a problem with ignorance or inconsiderate people, I know there is time to make more of a difference. I am not an incarnate angel, although I know quite a few, I am simply an old soul. So, here is to all of us who are on earth to make a difference at the cost of some of our time and energy, as we are generous givers of priceless gifts.

DIFFERENT PATHS & PERSONAL GROWTH

We all have a brain and we all have a mind. The difference is that we use our brains to physically function or to consider what we have learned. Our brains are chemically infused and cause us to feel certain ways, to love, hate, express, to talk, see, hear, feel, or move, you name it, everything we physically do comes from our brains. I must say there are days that my brain makes me love harder, despise stronger, and work longer, but without my mind, I am just a shell of a person. Basically, I am not Rebecca, rather I am a Being performing physical tasks, and considering the physical only with no spiritual, moral make-up, I have no character.

If I am not physically strong, I have no talents of strength, if I am not coordinated, I cannot dance, if I am tone-deaf, I cannot sing, if I am only considering what I know, then I cannot aspire to greater things. Everything outside of the physical is mental, and so goes the mind as it touches different planes of existence, people, energies, feelings, and resilience as we overcome some of the physical limitations of the brain and being human.

This drawing is of a woman named Carrie who was on her beach, mindful of the bees she was tending that could possibly sting her. They represented the people around her who might do just as much. Her husband sat on her be beach reading the paper, but not paying much attention to what she was doing. This represented his desire to be in her life, but not aware of what she was needing or going through. The tornado in the background was a representation of the chaos she was experiencing; however, she was actively pulling information from the tornado to build herself up.

To consider yourself almighty, with no influence from spirit or other unearthly beings is quite ignorant. Look at it this way. When you are trying to create something, you can use the information you know to come up with an idea, but there are times when you, all of a sudden, say I GOT IT!! That is one of those moments when Spirit is giving you a nudge in the right direction. Scientists invent based on knowledge and inspiration. Do you really think that Madam Curry discovered Radium and Polonium on her own or that Fleming just happened upon mold that cured infections? We are inspired to create, and hopefully we catch the cues and act. We can then use our brains to develop more, write more, create more, help more, and influence more.

Our brains help us to be logical, think critically, and weigh out decisions without emotional influence. Our brains work on what we know, have experienced, and want in ways of success, pleasure, and influence one direction or another, and usually it means ego and self are involved. Our minds work on what we feel from our hearts, with the exception of hormones that influence us physically through the brain. The unspoken feelings that we cannot explain. Our minds provide the means to emotionally, artistically, and sometimes irrationally handle situations. Our minds can sometimes be overstimulated by passion, drive, and innovation inspired by higher beings. And when God or Spirit inspires you to act, it is very hard to put that aside. On another note, you do not want to push aside anything inspired by God for Earthly or human reasons, because these are moments when we break free of human thinking and limitations. It is very hard to forget or ignore passion and inspiration, and if you do, you will probably regret it. Please do not confuse passion with lust though, because lust is not from God, whereas passion is heavenly.

People ask me, how do you do what you do? How can I do it too? The answer is quite simple, because everyone does it every day without trying. It is called daydreaming. When you are off in LaLa Land, you consciously shut off your rational thinking and allow all forms of possibility to enter your train of thought. Now you can see a problem or a limitation three-dimensionally. You can toss that problem or idea back and forth between you and a cartoon character if you so desired. There is nothing strange about it, because anything is possible while you are dreaming. What did I just say??!!!!! Holy snarkies!!!! Mind blown?! When we dream either while asleep or awake, we consciously shut off our brain's control of who and what we see, do and talk to. This is also where we talk to loved ones who have passed over, animals, God, Spirit, and 'ourselves,' and we allow crazy inspiration, words, and thoughts into our thinking patterns. We can see many things, and most people write these things off as their own incredible intelligence or they ignore them altogether. When you become really smart and figure something out, make sure you give credit where it is due, and you will always have that open line of communication right at a daydream.

Now let's say you are inspired to make a major change in your life, but that change means that you will make others uncomfortable. Your husband may have to make dinner twice a week or your children will have to stay with a sitter after school in order for you to take a new job. Or your wife will have to move away from her family so that you can take a dream job in another state. We all are faced with decisions that will rock not only our own worlds, but those of the people we love, and it is difficult to figure out what to do. Well, if I were reading for this person, I might see them standing on one side of a bridge, or in the shallow end of a stream, and both of those positions mean that this person has a big decision to make that involves comfort and making change. I can also tell you that positive change usually involves discomfort and growth, and all growing involves pains. Inspiration and messages come in many forms, and you may receive both negative and

positive messages, because like I said before, when you awaken to your purpose and path, you awaken to the knowledge that there are both light and dark beings around you, and they both have been working in your life this whole time, you are only just now aware of it. Only listen to the positive voices and messages.

Picture this, you are standing in a place that represents family, home, love, kids, happiness, contentment, dreams, or the lack of all these things. Once again, enter bridges, boulders, and rivers. Let's put you on one side of a bridge, which is the comfortable side of things, the known, experienced, lived side of the river. The bridge represents moving over a difficult transition, which is the water. The other side of the bridge is the risk, the opportunity, the change, or the desired way, but it can also be the side you must go to, but do not realize it because you are bombarded with difficulty, pain, loss, and fear. To reach the other side, a person must move from their comfort zone and across the bridge, but most of the time, they do this alone. We each have our own paths to complete, and we each must accomplish certain goals and tasks alone as well, which means that although people may be next to us, they are not experiencing our steps as we are experiencing them. These changes

This vision represented Jenna as she struggled to make a very uncomfortable decision of crossing a bridge that had to include her children. When we make decisions of any kind, they affect those around us, and here, she had to not only disrupt her own life, but those of her children as well. God has plans for us that we sometimes do not understand, and those require faith and trust that He will lead you properly.

mean they must find another way to meet you on the other side, and sometimes this trek is not in their hearts to make.

Sometimes a person is met with resistance from those they love in the way of guilt trips, fear of loss, or control. When someone is afraid that personal growth and success could cause their partner to see things differently, people can become jealous, controlling, or distant, all of which hurt and cause feelings of guilt, or that their choice to cross the bridge is wrong. I know that after all of these years reading for people, that crossing the bridge is a must. If someone is meant to stay in your life, they will find a way to make things work. If they are not, then it means there is nothing more to learn from that person and you have outgrown them. Some people are okay staying where they are, and that is okay; however, no one should ever stifle another person's growth and positive movement, simply because they are afraid of the outcome or cannot handle it. Always find people who support you. This does not mean being foolish or careless with others. It means that you could not consider ignoring a pathway for fear of personal regret. People should always be true to themselves, and one way to know you are making the right decision, is to pray to God, that His will be done in your life, and remove yourself and your ego from the entire deal. For instance, upon taking my abilities truly public, away from referrals only and into the social media world, my life was quite simple, albeit, I was going to school, having babies, and doing readings privately, it was simple. Everyone around me was quite comfortable with the way things were going; however, just the other day, about a year after deciding to make a go of my calling, my husband said, "You've been different for a long time. Just not you." I said I agreed, but not for the reasons he was implying. He believes that the 'things' that I attract were the main reason I was different, rather, they were only part of the issue. It was that I was changing, evolving, and following my path that God intended for me. I was making him uncomfortable.

It is very hard to choose a path that others disagree with, especially if you must live with them and they with you. It is difficult, because now everything is up for grabs and no one is sure of their roles. Give it time, and if it is meant to be, it will…simply put. Communication is most needed during these times, because if you are evolving according to your path, and you want to continue that path with those in your life, you must keep them abreast of what is going on. If a spouse or partner is changing and not including you in those changes, you need to ask why.

We all struggle with what is right or wrong, God's intention or destiny choice. We all struggle with what is best for us or best for others, how it affects us or the greater good, and we all must live with those free-will decisions as well. Sometimes we swallow the giant pill and keep going in the same direction, because we are not strong enough or we don't care enough to make the changes requiring that we walk alone. Some of us are just tired of fighting obstacles and give up on what we want. Is that fair? No. It is not. Those who love us should be supportive and happy that we are attempting to better ourselves, to grow, and become who God has intended. Those who fight change in their partners are afraid of *losing* their partners. Everyone knows when they are doing right and not doing right by others, and when you're not doing your best, you know in your heart you can be dumped or replaced when someone who is willing to do right by someone comes along. It is no one's job to carry you or lift you up, so figure things out and be who you *want* to be. Stop blaming others for failures and falls and recognize where you have short comings. Fix them. Fix yourself. And then ask to join the party so you don't miss out. One can only carry someone so long until they realize that the other person is no longer trying rather is dead weight. This is where jealousy and fear enter relationships, because one person is growing and the other still hasn't figured themselves out. Communication allows people to openly understand what each person is doing, decide if they are willing to work together to grow together, and forge ahead. A lack of communication combined with manipulations will cause discord. Just sayin. Figure out what you want and who you want it with and then communicate those desires to the people in your lives. A partner will either say, I want to join you on this journey or Meh, this isn't for me. Either way, you win.

Oh my gosh! How could I win if my partner walked away? Well… if they chose to grow with you, you would then figure out what needed to be done to include each other in parallel growth tracks. If your partner chose to exit the relationship because this was not where they saw themselves growing, then accept the loss of burden to accomplish what you needed, as carrying a hateful angry person on your journey would be too much to bear. Also realize that when you come to a junction where relationships end, that means someone else is coming along for you. Remember Joe and Marla…and then he met Mary. Also know that heartbreak is real. It is caused by a void of energy that we have grown accustomed too, and having that ripped away does cause pain, both physically and emotionally, so do not disregard those feelings, rather embrace them, acknowledge them, and in due time, set them free.

Let's look at this another way. You and your partner are sitting at the base of a giant boulder. You have your lawn chairs, fire pit, drinks, S'mores, umbrella, whatever floats your boat. You look up behind you and see a giant boulder...three stories tall. You say, "Hey! I'm going to climb that boulder! Do you want to go with me?" Your partner replies with a definite, No, so you stand up, brush off, and figure out how you plan on to tackle this monument. You start climbing, and you struggle at first, you break a few nails, you scrape your knee, and pull a muscle, but you are determined to make the trek. You continue to yell down at your partner about joining you, but they are very happy sitting there in their chair, drinking their drink, and relaxing as usual. You climb and climb, until you reach the top and you pull yourself over the edge. You can feel the cool grass, a welcome touch from the cold, hard rock that has been attempting to thrust you back down to the ground below.

You feel the warm breeze as brushes past your face and moves your hair out of your eyes...and you close them for that second of bliss as you realize you have conquered a great task in your life. You have completed a move that no one wanted to take with you or maybe you took a path that no one wanted to take *with* you. Either way you have just entered a new chapter and it can cause exhilaration and anxiety all at once, but what should we do? Cast all anxiety to God, because God does not cause anxiety…rather it is the shouts from the darker angels that cause us to turn around in fear. Do not let them win when you are so close to victory over restraint.

When you are moving in the right direction you will feel things. I want to give an example here that is very personal. I have always been a private person, and I have allowed my gift to travel through networks via word-of-mouth and referral. Two years ago, I heard, Rebecca, make this public. Take this to the people. Do what you have to do, and so I moved forward, uncomfortably for both myself and my family as I pursued the avenues to bring my gift to light. It has been very difficult to plan and push forward, because it has disrupted my family life and how we worked on a daily basis. I told my husband that I was going to continue going places and reaching people regardless if he supported me or not, and I was quite to the point and adamant that I could not let this go. I knew that God wanted me to reach as many people as possible and tell them about His presence in their lives. To tell them how loved they really are, and to ensure that they knew they were not alone. This meant spreading the knowledge that we have angels, guardians, archangels, and loved ones who had passed over all looking down on us. It meant telling people what it is like on the other side, how we get there, and how we choose to learn more by coming back to Earth. It meant explaining how leaving this life by our own hands affects us spiritually, and the impact it has our next life as we most surely will come back to right the wrong. I was directed to save people, and inform them about their purposes, struggles, blessings, views, perspectives…to enlighten them with the knowledge that they were so much more than just skin and bones.

The beauty of moving forward with my mission was not all easy though, never has been, regardless of how people view me. My path has been difficult, and it has been blocked by darker things that do not want me to succeed. I know this now, but I did not in the beginning, hence the want and desire to die, to commit suicide….to leave all of my family, friends, and future behind. Had I not realized why I was struggling, I would not be here to write this now, and you would not be reading. When we hear negative messages verbally or in our heads, it is real. I don't care what someone says…when you hear something, it is real! People listen to those words and voices, no matter if they are 100% competent or 100% deranged…. they listen. If you are hearing messages to stop what you are doing, and you know what you are doing is good work, and you are paired up with God to do them, then know you should NOT listen to them. People and dark energies will be set in your way to turn you away from your Godly goal. They will tell you that you are dumb for attempting something new or stupid for thinking something so great could even be possible. Well, Moses was just one man and look at what he did with God's help and guidance.

When you are passionate about something and you are moving forward with a divine plan, I can almost guarantee at some point you will hear words or messages that cause you to rethink your plan or even quit altogether. In my case, I felt guilt for always being gone, for missing my kids, for making my kids miss me, and for causing my husband to worry about us as a couple. I felt guilty that I was not there to make dinners or kiss my family goodnight. I felt guilty that my time at home as also very busy and I seemed to always be working. Then I remembered that when you are close to achieving God's plan, the devil says, instill some guilt, fear and low self-confidence to stop her, and make her feel less worthy or incapable, to make a fool of herself. With that I knew I was doing God's work, because why else would the devil want me to stop? I knew I had to take the talents God had given me and push through all the negatives being thrown at me. I had to understand my family and what they were going through, and also consider the need for attention and extra love and compassion as I pursued this unknown path.

We all have times when we want to do something or we feel we must attempt to climb the unknown boulder, not because we have great faith in ourselves, but because we have great faith in the push to do so. I sit here and imagine being a person who has little to no faith, overcome with a push and desire to attempt some crazy feat, only to discover the immense blessings and understanding that come from achievement....that moment when you realize there is something Greater out there guiding each of us. Oh, how amazing that first time must be. I know how it feels with each subsequent occurrence, and it is always amazing.

So, to close my story, I want to also explain, that when I climbed that boulder, and left my family at the base, I had a choice to include them or not. I chose to include my family in my growth and then allow them to accept that invitation or not. My husband chose to learn more about what I do, to grow with me, and to show his support. I was lucky, because not all spouses and partners do that, rather they sit comfortably at the base while their other half goes on to discover and get lost in their new adventures. You can only imagine what happens. My family takes part in my events, my travels, and my pursuits, and we work together as a family, learning with one another. It is an amazing blessing. Now, not to change the subject or anything, but I feel the need to bring up the Jack-of-all-Trades persona as well. The person who is never quite satisfied with their path, gets bored easily, and is good at many things…that person. Usually these people are not here for themselves, and fall into the old soul category, and I bring them up here due to the chapter being about different paths. These people are chameleons with the ability to be who they need to be in any given moment to fulfill a need. They interchange lifestyles and personas, statuses, and abilities easily and do so with ease. This is effortless, because they truly have a gamut of previous lives under their belts they can relate to and quickly understand who and what is needed in any given situation to make things work.

These people I can pick up and put in a cabin in the North woods all by themselves or dress them in black tie and tails and drop them in on a dinner party at 5th and Broadway in New York: They always get along. People are attracted to them, because of their ability to make things look easy, even if they aren't, and their savvy, quick thinking is attractive as well. These people naturally draw attention to themselves as the person to call in a bind, and always seem to have the answer or ability to smooth things over. The ability to listen and respond eloquently and intelligently makes them excellent doctors, lawyers, and counselors. Their compassion levels are quite high due to the extensive list of lives behind them, some good and some a struggle. These people are prone to compassion burnout though and need to tend to themselves often, because as high as they can soar, they can doubly dive low. They care more about others than themselves, and this puts them into energy depletion quite often. The Jack-of-all-Trades soul can do just about anything, and is good at many things, never truly settled on one career, rather constantly learning and growing, sometimes viewed as the entrepreneur or dreamer type. We need these people, because they appear in jams, clear up troubles, and move on. They are earth angels of sorts, and although many of us play the role of earth angel in people's lives, this is simply the path of the Jack-of-all-trades. Always looking for the next exciting career, good at much, desired, and loved by many.

There are so many types of souls in the world, all of us learning and growing, some awakening anew, and some having understood their paths from childhood. All of us are here to support one another to become better people. We are not sent here to fight about skin color, or gender issues, or who to vote for, as these are man made issues. We are here to look past what man would have us quarrel about and see the beauty of each soul. I am not saying that people are not afraid of man-made issues, because we are; however, it is easy to look past those issues as well. What do you think would happen if we all covered ourselves up and wore paper bags on our heads? If we all physically looked the same...then what? What excuses would we have to dislike one person over another? I am sure man would create the issue.

Follow your path. Be true to your heart and to God. Ignore the nay-sayers and those who would stop you on your path or growth. Bless one another by being the blessing. Give of your heart, time, and energy. Shut off negative energy cycles and pathways, and don't let them exist around you (easier said than done, but worth a try). Include others. Invite others. We all have different pathways, but we all walk parallel to each other.

ANGELS

You cannot see. You attempt to open your eyes, but they are full of a goopy goo that makes it near impossible. You hear laughter, coos, and awes, as images move through your visual points. Through the loud, near voices you hear a gentle whisper "Mary......Maaaarrry." We all go through the same thing. All races, creeds, and religions experience the same event in order to get here. We are all pulled into existence, cold, fresh and new. We all are brethren. How? Because we all have the same celestial starting point. Hard to believe in a time of such distance and segregation, and not to get off on a different track, but I see the same elements, and energies for Christians, Muslims, Buddhists, Catholics, Protestants, Methodists, Lutherans, Chinese, Japanese, Jewish, Black, White, Yellow, gay, straight, bi, questioning, and so on. We are all the same. Accept it.

Okay, where were we.

As you lie in your mother's arms, you are unknowingly visited by your Archangel. This angel has been with you *all* of your lives. Depending on how many you have lived, maybe you're a new soul...maybe you have lived 50 lives, nevertheless, your archangel knows everything about who you *have* been, who you *are*, and who you are *going* to be. Standing with your Archangel are about six guardian angels. I say *about*, because I have only seen up to six around a person who is in a lot of trouble or at a point of great need.

Your Archangel stands next to you and says to the angels, "This is Mary. She has a plan to succeed. She is very special, and God loves her very much. He has shown Mary her path, and she has much to do while she is here. What I need you to do is lift her up when she is afraid or down. Whisper to her the guidance she needs when she is uncertain. Provide her the support she needs to stay on her path. Make her laugh. Dry her tears. Fill her heart with warmth. Love her always. That is your job while she is here. But remember that you cannot make her do anything. You cannot make her forgive, or love, or open her heart. You cannot make her choose, or change, or see a point. You cannot make her do anything, as God's gift to her is free will; however, you may inspire her to act. He has written a contract with her about what she wants to learn, what He wants her to learn, what she needs to learn, and what He wants her to do in terms of talents and skills; however, she as the ability to choose one path or another. He has allowed her the ability to think, and reason, and decide for herself. Hope that she asks for Wisdom and Discernment as she grows to help her with her trials. This is your job while she is here." The angels are excited and cheer for Mary, and then accept their duties while they are guiding and guarding her. Mary will never go anywhere without them.

There cannot be light without dark, as dark is the absence of light, thus they both exist. As there are Light Archangels, and Light Spiritual Guardian Angels, there is also the devil and his dark angels. You may laugh, but the devil is real. I call him the devil, but he may be known to you as Satan, the Evil One, Lucifer, Beelzebub or simply an energy that is dark and evil. The devil stands on your left with his dark angels and says, "This is Mary. She has a plan to succeed. She is very special, and God loves her very much. He has shown Mary her path, and she has much to do while she is here. What I need you to do is shake her self-belief when she is inspired and passionate. Speak loudly to her that she is not strong enough to complete a new task, especially if she is confident in herself. You must remove that certainty. Provide her with temptations and distractions that pull her from her tasks and path. Make her uncertain of which direction to go. Show her possibilities so she doubts her intuition and self. When she is sad, kick her. When she is feeling defeated, kick her harder. Make her cry. Wet her cheeks with fear and a feeling of being unloved. Fill her heart with discouragement. That is your job while she is here. But remember that you cannot make her do anything. You cannot make her hate, but you can speak to her and make her feel hated. You can inspire her to feel hate. You cannot make her choose, or change, or see a point, but you can fill her head with enough voices that she believes them to be her own. You cannot make her do anything, as God's gift to her is free will. He has written a contract with her about what she wants to learn, what He wants her to learn, what she needs to learn, and what He wants her to do in terms of talents and skills; however, she as the ability to choose one path or another. He has allowed her the ability to think, and reason, and decide for herself. This is where we come in, because we want her to choose to end this life. With that choice comes the destruction of other lives she won't help, save, or bring into this world. We will succeed in making her think she is crazy, no good, or of no use to those around her. Hope that she lacks the Wisdom and Discernment to help her with her trials. This is your job while she is here." The darker angels cheer and accept their duties while Mary exists. She will never be without these dark angels.

This proverbial angel/devil cartoon characters are very real, and we all have the same scene playing out every second of every day of the rest of our lives from birth until death. Like I had shared earlier, we

have this spiritual warfare happening from the moment we are born, and probably before that since we are much older than we realize. When people do not realize that this is a legitimate happening, or they are more focused on themselves and the Earthly events occurring around them, then this can become dangerous, because they believe the things that they hear to be coming from themselves. What do I mean by hear?

When we daydream, think deeply, fantasize, or imagine, we are allowing our brains to think outside the 'box.' We are saying, I am going to think hypothetical and crazy things here so don't shut me down. In this instance, you are saying that anything is possible. We leave the confines of our brains, of what we know, of what we conceive to be real or true, and we fly through space, time, and ideas. We turn off the subconscious 'bouncer' that says, you cannot do that! You cannot enter here, and we gleefully see what could be and also…what truly is. This is where our loved ones, our angels, and our demons find us, and it is where we hold deep conversations of understanding and consciousness. We turn off the barrier to taking a walk with our favorite movie star and we fly through the stars on a magic carpet…. anything is possible while daydreaming.

This is the place where I read. It is the place I go, that I have trained myself to enter almost immediately that allows me to read people near and far, here and there. It is the place where I know demons also exist and which directions and voices not to listen to as they are false. Everyone has this place, this ability, this knowledge, and it simply means tuning in and trusting. The best information comes from this place, because it usually steers you in the right direction, if it is positive, good information.

If you are thinking anything, it doesn't matter what or who it is about, if you are thinking something and it comes out negatively or wrapped in hate or anger, it is not from you. Do not listen to it. For instance, you are thinking of Janet, and Janet has upset you with a lie. While thinking of Janet you say to yourself, I am so mad at Janet, she really hurt me, and then you hear, "You should tell her off! Tell her what you are feeling and thinking and make her feel just as badly", then you can rest assured that it is not coming from a Godly source, rather the other. If you hear, "you are fat, ugly, unwanted, no one loves you, and no one cares if you are here", then you can also trust that it is not from a Godly source, as our angels will never make us feel badly or hurt us. Realize that when you are in a place of angels, there is both light and dark, just as there are two sides of every story, person, fence or spectrum…there's always more.

If you focus on the negative messages, visions, aspects, and ideas, then you will only reap negative, and that is what the darker angels are hoping for…that you will not be able to discern the difference, believe what you hear to be yourself, and then move forward with negative plans of action based on those visions and voices. You must listen for the quiet whispers that come from the heavenly source. They are harder to hear and sometimes harder to understand, but they are true and correct, and they would not lead you astray. We wrestle with these voices and argue with them, but they are real, and it is not a coincidence or an impossibility. You are talking to your 'cricket', your conscience, and it just so happens that through that voice you hear your angels, God, those passed over, and the darker ones.

It is hard to follow sometimes, because as humans we seek the pleasure principle, the gratification, and the 'feeling' rather than the spiritual growth, the lesson or the sense of what's right. It is difficult to discern these voices if you are upset or angry, and most of the time it is easier to listen to the upset, angry, jealous, hateful voices we hear rather than those that are forgiving, compassionate, and loving. I know firsthand and I have been known to look up and roll my eyes when I hear "Rebecca! Be nice!" Especially when the other person or people are not being nice. It can be hard to stand back and find compassion for their behavior, but it is possible, it just takes practice. I also want to add here that there are people I do not like...go figure...but there are people I knowingly would not be friends with, but these same people I would sit down with and read for them, allowing God to pass His messages through to them. When this has happened...yes it has happened many times, I see people I don't like through God's eyes and heart, and it can change mine. I appreciate this happening, as I learn so much.

This is what leads me to what can happen if you listen to the darker voices, or the ones that tell you to do what you know in your heart is the wrong choice. It could be anything from, go ahead and eat the cookie, when you're on a diet, to, no one wants you around anyway, so just do It. Like I explained before, there are forces here to help and guide us properly, but there are those here to sabotage and guide us improperly as well. Both have a purpose to fulfill for different reasons, and through both we all learn lessons, some of which, once learned, you cannot choose otherwise later.

Understanding that angels are among us can help you with your day in simple ways. It can make a difference how you treat people. It can make you take a second look at the people you deal with on a daily basis, allowing yourself a chance to take a look at who someone is, what they are dealing with, and what their purpose is. I know this sounds funny, but I have to add this too. During my doctoral education, I had several professors with very opposite perspectives of mine, they tended to lean hard one direction and they could not be swayed any other. I quickly realized how I had to present my work in order to get a good grade, because anything other than the professor's viewpoint was wrong. I am quite outspoken, especially when it comes to justice and what is right, and I got into a tiff with several at the possibility of getting a very low grade (I graduated Summa Cum Laude), and those professors whom I had such a hard time with eventually became some of the people I came to admire and emulate. So, when people hold you to something, and keep you doing what is right, even if you don't understand it yet, you may find they are leading you correctly. I still say their points-of-view are messed up though, but their teaching styles kept me on my toes.

Angels come in many forms. Always do what is right when it is right. Stick up for the little guy. Don't be a bully. Speak your mind, but not to hurt someone else. Shield the underdog and take them under your wings. Give often even if you get nothing in return. Keep your head up and your eyes open. Smile at everyone. Make eye contact and say hello no matter their race, dress, status, or wealth. Hold doors and say thank you when someone holds one for you. Pay for the person behind you at the drive-through. Carry someone's bag. Hug someone. Hold someone. Smile at the reflection in the mirror. All of these things are priceless, and you never know whose life you may change. Consider this. Joe wakes up one morning and he is devastated that he just lost his job and his wife left him days before. He looks in the mirror in disgust and hates the reflection. He cries. He is defeated and feeling hopeless at the thought of having to start over with his life. He looks up and says, "God! If you want me to stay here…. if you really want me to stay here, then let me know! Give me a sign that you want me here! That I matter at all to you! Let's see how mighty and powerful you are…. If one person looks me in the eyes and says Hello to me, then I will take that as a sign to stay." Keep in mind that God cannot be tempted, nor does He ever act on command, but He can inspire us. When I am out, I consider this very thought, and when someone makes eye contact with me, I smile…and say hello. You just never know whose life you are going to change, and to that one person…you became a lifesaving, message-bearing angel.

SUICIDE

Taking one's own life is a trauma that all those around the victim feel, but I don't leave it at only those who knew the person, because with social media abounding, anyone who reads about suicide is saddened by the loss of life. It is a reverberation of energy waves blowing through the cosmos as a soul ceasing to exist, and the ending of one's life causes profuse pain as that wave is felt. I want to put it out there early though, that not all those who have committed suicide, whom I have spoken with, were sorry about what they did; however, the majority of them are sad and regretful of what they did the moment the accomplished what they set out to do.

Suicide seems to be a more and more common happening. I cannot express the number of suicides that I have heard about recently. It seems like two or three a week are at my attention, not to mention the people who come to me asking if I can talk to someone who has committed suicide. As a servant of the Lord it kills me every time I hear about a suicide, and I break down. It is frustrating because I am only one person, and no matter how many Youtube videos I do, I can only reach so many. And still, so many who listen are so caught up in their issues that they don't want to or cannot focus on the spiritual aspect of things.

A video can only do so much, and who knows what people are actually doing or thinking when they watch them.

It appears through comments and private contacts from many that they have lost sight of God and are wandering through this world wondering where they belong, to whom they belong, and why. They exist. They breath. They hear only what their mind tells them, or so they think. Consider back now to the moment you were born and assigned your angels for support in this life, and also consider the darker angels that were assigned to follow you to the end. When we are down, the dark angels see the anguish, desperation, sadness, tears, fear, hurt, pain, loss, or whatever is bringing that person down, and they gang up like ants on cotton candy. Devouring the person, their soul, and their hope until there is nothing left but a few remainders of what used to be. When a soul is depleted, it is easier to swallow, and this is the aim of the darker angels, the demons. A person who has lost sight of God, has lost their anchor. They are floating aimlessly in a vast ocean of nothing-on-the-horizon. God does not walk away from us; we walk away from Him.

Imagine being at a fair at the age of 5 and losing your parents. You're looking up at strange faces and you are surrounded by legs, torsos, and pushing bodies. You are scared, lost, and afraid. You know that feeling of what a backyard looks like as an adult compared to when you were a child? The size of something as a child is immense and your little legs can run for what seems miles, only to see a shrunken version of the same as an adult. Imagine again…in this instance, how huge this fair just became, and then out of nowhere, a person comes along and says, are you lost little girl? Do you need help? What do you do? Who do you trust? Imagine if this person had ill-intentions, now what? You're screwed if you cannot find your parents. This is what bad people and bad energies do…they thrive upon lost souls and those who would ask for help. Would you go somewhere with a stranger? No. Then make sure you only listen to those who have your best interests at heart, which means they would not tell you to do something to harm yourself, others, or sabotage something good in your life, and regardless of how long you have been away from your parents, you still recognize them.

Now life is funny sometimes and ironic how timing happens, but as I am typing this right now, a friend of mine just sent me a message on my cell telling me that her Godson committed suicide last night by hanging. He was 13. I am typing through blurry eyes right now, because it is another soul lost, and I know what they go through when they commit this act. I cannot see him. I cannot connect with him any other way other than he is afraid. I am broken-hearted for my friend, for her Godson, and for their family, as so much is left unfinished, and so many questions are left unanswered.

When you can no longer handle things on your own...this is when you let go and say, "God, please tie my shoes. I cannot do this. I do not know how. I have tried and tried in my own way and it never works. I will let you tie my shoes now." Notice the "I will," because you are finally giving *your* will to Him. I say a prayer every day that God's will be done before mine. That 'I' be removed from the equation because I do not fully understand my path and 'I' may make a mistake in deciding based on my will or ego. This prayer removes the strain from me to make the right decisions, and I know regardless of how it turns out, that it is the right path for me. It is quite awesome to live like that, because it means you accept the good, bad, fun, boring, and teachable. Know that regardless of how long you have been away from 'home,' your Father in Heaven always leaves the Light on for you.

I don't want to explain away the reasons as to why people commit suicide, because there are physical reasons, chemical reasons, and emotional reasons that can take over a person, mind, body, and soul. When a person sees no end to pain, no resolution to a problem, no way to reclaim what is lost, they can be overcome with grief, defeat, self-loathing, or disgust. I am saddened by this happening, and consider it part of my purpose to help people out of the dark, muddy, cold holes they find themselves in. I know I cannot save everyone, rather I lead as many as I can to the path to being saved. If you ever find yourself here, take a nap. Go to sleep. See what happens by the time you wake up.

I do this work, because I once sat in a bathtub, unable to see through the tears and swollen eyes caused by the agony of daily panic attacks that I suffered alone. I had had enough pain and terror and could no longer understand why I was suffering. Why I was losing my mind. Why I was incapable of controlling this desperate need to run and escape my body, mind, and life. I cried to the Heavens, and I begged God for relief and the strength to help me. I prayed for guidance, and I told Him I no longer wanted to be here. It was a sad time, and no one knew I was so tormented. In my head was a thousand voices, all telling me that I should just die. During this time, I also want to add, that I had all but quit my readings for people. I walked away from guiding others, from receiving messages from God, and from generally helping God's people. I was utterly alone.

That night, while my husband and children were downstairs watching television, I cried my heart out. I bowed down and ultimately prostrated myself. I felt I had to go as low as possible in order to receive any message or reply from God. I heard…Get your bible Rebecca, and I did…again through blurred, tear-filled eyes. I held it by the spine, and I asked for His advice, for His help, and I let the book fall open. I looked down to see 1 Peter 4:

Therefore, since Christ suffered in his body, arm yourselves also with the same attitude, because whoever suffers in the body is done with sin.² As a result, they do not live the rest of their earthly lives for evil human desires, but rather for the will of God. ³ For you have spent enough time in the past doing what pagans choose to do—living in debauchery, lust, drunkenness, orgies, carousing and detestable idolatry. ⁴ They are surprised that you do not join them in their reckless, wild living, and they heap abuse on you. ⁵ But they will have to give account to him who is ready to judge the living and the dead. ⁶ For this is the reason the gospel was preached even to those who are now dead, so that they might be judged according to human standards in regard to the body but live according to God in regard to the spirit. ⁷ The end of all things is near. Therefore, be alert and of sober mind so that you may pray. ⁸ Above all, love each other deeply, because love covers over a multitude of sins. ⁹ Offer hospitality to one another without grumbling. ¹⁰ Each of you should use whatever gift you have received to serve others, as faithful stewards of God's grace in its various forms. ¹¹ If anyone speaks, they should do so as one who speaks the very words of God. If anyone serves, they should do so with the strength God provides, so that in all things God may be praised through Jesus Christ. To him be the glory and the power for ever and ever. Amen.

Suffering for Being a Christian

[12] Dear friends, do not be surprised at the fiery ordeal that has come on you to test you, as though something strange were happening to you. [13] But rejoice inasmuch as you participate in the sufferings of Christ, so that you may be overjoyed when his glory is revealed. [14] If you are insulted because of the name of Christ, you are blessed, for the Spirit of glory and of God rests on you. [15] If you suffer, it should not be as a murderer or thief or any other kind of criminal, or even as a meddler. [16] However, if you suffer as a Christian, do not be ashamed, but praise God that you bear that name. [17] For it is time for judgment to begin with God's household; and if it begins with us, what will the outcome be for those who do not obey the gospel of God? [18] And, "If it is hard for the righteous to be saved, what will become of the ungodly and the sinner?" [19] So then, those who suffer according to God's will should commit themselves to their faithful Creator and continue to do good.

When I read this short chapter in 1 Peter, I bawled like a baby, silently so no one could hear me. I cried upward and into my hands. I let go of every suffering I had been carrying, because I then realized that I was not the only one suffering, and that I *was* being tormented. I knew in that moment that God had heard my prayer, and that I no longer would suffer, because I knew I was a Child of God, and that He wanted me to live. He wanted me to forgive myself, which is so very hard, and he wanted me to know that I had to use my gifts to help others, and that I had suffered in the body for two years, a humbling, crippling experience that I wish upon no one. Had I given in to the voices that tempted me to leave this life, I would have missed out on more than can explain. I would have let three souls to figure out a new way to be born. I would have left my husband with the burden of raising children alone, having to explain to them why their mother was not there, and why she didn't love them enough to figure out her issues. I would have missed all the people I have met since then, and as I type right now...it would have been nine years of a wonderful life gone, as well as the many more to come...I hope.

I was saved that day. I was saved in so many ways, and my faith was increased 10-fold. I am not a religious person by any means, but I know God has my back. I know Jesus has my hand and at times He carries me when I can no longer walk the walk. This is the same for all of God's children, I am not special by any means, and I want everyone reading this to know how it really is. I hope that everyone has that moment when they meet God in this life, because it is quite amazing, and it reveals much to the mind and heart. Understand that while God is present and immovable and provides us with guidance and wisdom, there are always the darker energies that attempt to bring people down and remove all hope for the ability to stand again. They whisper and present like your own voice in your head, and they mock your pain, by repeating over and over the worries, losses, and defeats you believe define your life at that moment.

You are worthy of every lesson that comes your way. You deserve every blessing that presents to you. You are here for a reason, even though you may not understand why. You are loved by more souls and hearts that you recognize. Shut out every negative voice you hear and tell yourself five positive things about you, your life, and your dreams. This tends to take time, and the more time you think positively, the better you are at hearing God.

ANXIETY

This is the chapter that I pondered back and forth actually writing. I don't even think I will call it a chapter at this point because I don't know if it will even be long enough to be considered a chapter. I want to write about this though, because I feel that it will at least answer a few questions for people, and because it has come up repeatedly in the past few weeks. I want to start off with saying that there are people who have clinical, physical depression and anxiety symptoms and repercussions. I am in no way saying that you should not take your prescribed medications, or that you should not see a doctor, or that you should stop seeing a doctor; however, I am staying that there may be more to feelings and happenings than meets the eye or that can be diagnosed medically.

I want to add that if you are dealing with anxiety it is most likely that you are also dealing with a depression or depressive state. I do not want you rushing to decisions, I simply want to ensure you know you are not crazy, and that other explanations are out there. Something to consider while you are being treated or if you decide to get into treatment is the fact that we are spiritual beings that are affected by spiritual things. We have emotions that are affected chemically, hormonally, energetically, physically, spiritually, psychically, and emotionally. You cannot discount the fact that there is something else going on if you are reading this book. Ideally, we would be able to go to one folder and find everything we needed, but that's just never the case, so why would anyone expect to find all of the solutions in one folder? Why would anyone expect to find all of the ingredients in one place? In order to create something, we sometimes have to look in other places where different things are kept.

Let's start off with this, and I am using an example from a friend of mine. You are 40 years old and you are sitting in a doctor's office about to get an MRI, and everything is fine, your day is great. You get into the MRI machine, you lay back, and they slide you into a tiny tunnel and all of a sudden, your heart starts pounding, and you are now short of breath and panicking because you're in an enclosed place. This doesn't just happen out of the blue. Experiences like panic and anxiety can be triggered my previous life experiences such as drowning, fires, being caved in, abandonment, loss, sickness, and many other things. If you die in a previous life due to a traumatic experience, you can very well bring that residual issue with to this life, possibly to get through it this time, work through any trauma, or simply carry it on. Discovering that you have a new anxiety caused such an event as entering an MRI machine is cause enough to attempt to figure out why you may be suffering all of a sudden from such a simple and minor experience.

If you have trauma from a past life, it is very possible that you have brought that residual energy along with you this time and it may strike you without notice causing you to wonder what is wrong with you. If you cannot figure it out, it can plague you and make you feel mad, crazy, suicidal, and hopeless.

Nothing is worse that anxiety, fight or flight, without reasoning, because you feel like you have nowhere to go, run or turn. Recognizing that something has just started and was triggered by an event, can help you to understand that it may be past life related, and allow you a chance to get the right help from someone who understands past lives, and past life regressions. If you face anxiety long enough on your own, it can cause depression, phobias, and co-morbid psychological issues. Do not simply attempt to get medical/psychological help, rather, couple your treatment with spiritual access and guidance, because you may find that you are not crazy, clinically depressed or schizophrenic, instead, you are highly tuned in to your spiritual self and what is going on this time around. A good medium or spiritualist can tell the difference, and

This is a vision of a man who was drowning in his perceived problems. He was head under water and struggling. The buoy represented God's presence in his life. It showed that all he had to do was find his way to God and God would save him from sinking any deeper. It was quite an amazing visual.

believe me, if you came to me with a demon on your back, or spiritual connections, I will tell you what is going on, but I will also tell you if you need medical intervention as well to help

you out. There is just too much going on here to explain, and each person is different. I just want to make sure that people understand that there is more to us than a brain and chemicals.

I would also like to point out that if you are sensitive to energies, you may also sense and feel when something attaches to you, be it while you're watching a baseball game or you're at Walmart. Once an attachment happens it can draw all of your energy away and make you feel hypoglycemic or panicky. It creates an energy depletion and exhaustion, as well as the shakes, weakness, sweating, and tingly. For these reasons, I eat food, sugars, and maintain a full stomach when doing readings and investigations so I know that if an attachment occurs, it is for certain not low-blood sugar. I also know to kick into protective mode and ward energies off with prayer and light protection, all of which I do in Christ's light and using Archangel Michael's assistance. There are many resources you can find online about this, and I am more than happy to do more educational events on this as well, so do not hesitate to reach out to me in mind that any true healer, will help you without payment, so don't spend an arm and a leg getting spiritual help.

Understand that anxiety can come from current life and past life situations, and little things can trigger emotions you may not understand. Anxiety can come from the fear of dying young again as you may have in a past life, and it may be that you lost all of your family and dealt with life alone, feeling abandoned and now, upon the knowledge of losing a parent, you start to have panic attacks and are not sure why. Understand that life events can trigger those fears and insecurities, especially if they fall around the same age as they happened previously. The best thing to do, is to acknowledge what is going on, take a deep breath, and remind yourself that this is not a lesson in this life, you simply have to get through this short time. But again, as I stated, anxiety can be caused by several spiritual components and happenings and reaching out to a spiritualist may help. And just so we're clear, a spiritualist understands past lives, how souls live forever, and spiritual happenings, some of which is not accepted by the medical field or certain religions. Just remain open.

ONE HUMANITY. ACCEPTANCE NOT TOLERANCE

"When you reach a level of acceptance rather than tolerance, you evolve to another spiritual level." – Dr. Rebecca Foster

We all have our preconceived notions about people, places, and things, and those prejudices can hinder our experiences in life. As a university instructor, I have found that one of the most important aspects of learning is supporting your assertions. I cannot express to my students enough that if they are going to teach me something, they had better support it with factual and scholarly sources. Do not tell me that all companies do something this way or that all people prefer red over blue phones, without showing me where you got this information. If I can ask, how do you know that, then there had better be a reference and citation to show me the research and support for that statement or assertion; otherwise, it is simply an opinion or assumption.

I cannot tell you how many times I personally have stated something and thought to myself that I needed to research my opinion, only to find out that I was very wrong. I was also very thankful that I took the time to look something up before I ran my mouth. Opinions, assertions, and statements are only beliefs until they are supported by factual reality.

The same goes for what and how we think. If you believe that all White people follow Hitler or that all Black people commit crimes, then you are ignorant, not so much a racist or bigot, just more ignorant than anything. If you believe that all Jews are rich and run Hollywood, you are ignorant. If you believe that all Mexicans living in America are illegals, then you are ignorant. Too much is put out there anymore about racism…yes it exists, and racism is alive, but it centers around ignorance. Teach the facts, and ignorance is removed. Get to know something or someone in-depth rather than off of social media and you remove ignorance. If a factual lesson has been expressed and taught, and people still choose to behave like Neanderthals, then yes, they are probably racist, but most of the time, they are just ignorant. And please, let's define ignorant…if I pull the definition from Bing Search, I get, "lacking knowledge or awareness in general; uneducated or unsophisticated, discourteous or rude, and insensible, unconscious, and lacking knowledge, information, or awareness about a particular thing." Ignorant means that someone doesn't know what they heck they are talking about or doing.

I believe that ignorance applies to more people than not, because in today's society, people can get online, hide behind computers, and rant in any way they feel like letting off steam at that moment. This means that they will probably say and do stupid things they might not otherwise do, especially in person. I have had my own growth that I have had to overcome, simply based on my own experiences that have created prejudices. I am not a racist, nor do I hate any religion, race, or creed. I have feelings about particular people based on how they have treated me, and I am sure you have as well. These events do not mean that we can call out a whole group based on one person's behaviors, and I know we all feel the same way.

So, let me get to the title of this chapter…Acceptance not Tolerance. I for one do not want to be around people that I have to tolerate, because that is one of the most unpleasant things to do. Consider holidays with family…Holy Cows, they can be insufferable depending on who is going to be attending a party or get together. You might even find yourself getting ill just anticipating the event. Tolerating people or simply one person is no fun, and it can really ruin a moment, a day, a week, or a lifetime.

Tolerating someone, a neighbor, a community, a people, a country, a religion, a gender or any group at all is baggage that can be quite heavy. With tolerance comes suppressed anger, hurt, pain, sadness, anxiety, and possibly depression. With tolerance comes a fake smile, talking under your breath, seething emotions, and disdain. When you simply tolerate someone, you are not living. You are not happy. You are not enjoying all those moments. Letting go of tolerance is one of the best things we as humans can do. Acceptance is what we need to embrace.

Tolerance is putting up with someone while feeling all the emotions of not liking them. This just makes me want to throw up thinking about the anxiety attack that could ensue. Accepting someone means that you are allowing who a person to be who they are without attempting to change them. It means that you do not agree with them, but at the same time you just don't care. And it's not that you don't care about something, it means you have released the will and desire to change, erase, or dwell on it. It means you have gained the perspective and initiative that you are going to do your thing regardless of who else is there or is taking part. It means that no one else controls your happiness in that moment, or any moments for that matter. It means that you are going to laugh as loud as you can without worrying about embarrassing anyone else. Acceptance releases you from feeling anything about another person, their lifestyle, or their personal being. Believe me, this can be hard, and I can say that I have spent many holidays tolerating people and I can guarantee they have done with same with me. The tension is usually quite thick, but once you stop focusing on what you dislike or find at odds, then you quickly realize how much you can enjoy a moment you otherwise might have turned down.

I have found myself in several positions of having to endure a certain person or persons because of obligation, or because someone I might not agree with is enjoyed by someone I love. This is putting others first, and it is one of the hardest things to do. I cannot say I have done so gracefully in each instance, but I do not make people feel uncomfortable either. I must admit though, that there are times I am out and about and an employee of an establishment that I am patronizing is rude, and I do not tolerate it at all. I usually call them out on their behavior, because some people just need to be woken up to the energy they are exuding. Asking the simple question, are you having a bad day, or did I do something to upset you, is usually enough to stop someone in their tracks. I also want to point out that no one should tolerate being mistreated.

Do not accept being mistreated, because as humans, we are all on the same playing field, just some are in different walks of life, but none are better. Some may be better at hiding their problems, issues, and faults, but none of us are better. The moment you judge someone for doing something is a moment you won't soon forget, because like I have said before, God has a way of teaching us compassion the hard way.

Let's look at the word 'tolerate.' It means to endure something or someone unpleasant, and it also means to endure subjection to something or someone such as a drug, alcohol, or a negative person. No one should have to endure or be subject to anyone or anything. No one should accept negative, hateful, demeaning behaviors from others, so I am not saying that you should accept or tolerate them in the least. What I am saying, is if you are upset by a person based on color, status, religion, political affiliation, history, gender, who they love, or what they love, then move on. Who are you to judge? This is a sensitive subject and one I am passionate about, because no one should judge or be judged. NO one is perfect, and no one has it all together. We are all human. Accepting someone for being human is a way to start. I will not be a hypocrite though and say I do not have opinions on politics and religion, because I do. I cannot believe some of the things that people say and spread, but again, it all comes down to ignorance.

I feel badly for people who do not fully understand what they are putting out there on social media or the news, or in the papers. I shake my head and wonder what is this world coming to? I want to help those people, but ignorance is truly bliss. Ohhhhh, Rebecca's judging people....!!! No. I'm not. I am stating a fact. Ignorance leads to many issues. If you get the facts for yourself, and you gain knowledge and understanding, then you too can help the situations by leading, by following your own drummer, or by simply standing up for what is right. But what's right? All I can say, is each person has their own perspective, and if you can live with yourself at night, and you are not suffering from anxiety over your own behaviors, then you must be doing something right. It takes many people to make up this world, and with many people comes many different opinions, ideas, perspectives, and beliefs. We are all different. We love differently. We pray differently. We learn differently. We behave differently, raise our children differently, speak differently, and present differently. Why on earth would be all want to be the same? God forbid we were all the same.

Accepting God's work in all of us is what acceptance is, and judging others means you are questioning God's will. I want to say though…that stupidity is not an option in this time. We have too many resources to be educated to act ignorantly and stupidly. Let me leave you with this…if I were to be given a room filled with people, all dressed in blue t-shirts and jeans with white sneakers, I would read them all differently. AND I would see them as God sees them, with love, hope, beauty, potential, fears, and courage, regardless if I was reading an avid churchgoer, or a person facing life in prison. That is the beauty of my gift…seeing people as they are on the inside. I don't care how I disagree with someone, once I see their soul…I see love. (Unless you're just a jerk and there is no reaching you, then I just walk away from the connection.) Decide if you are tolerating someone, being around them, their presence, or even that of a job or career choice. Open up to the idea of why you may be miserable and honestly look at the situation and how you fit into everything. Do not make a rash and hasty decision, because you may just be having a bad day and are frustrated by goings-on. When I was pregnant, I would want to cut my hair off, because it was long and hard to deal with, but my hairdresser would not allow it. She would tell me point-blank that I was hormonal. I appreciated her advice.

If you are tolerating someone or something, then step back from the scenario. Try to see them or it for what it could be beyond the surface, and open yourself up to God's love, asking for it and the Holy Spirit to flow through you. Ask for wisdom in an intolerable situation. Ask for discernment and guidance to see things for what they are outside of your own temporal belief. You may find, against your human judgement, that you can actually accept some of the things you truly dislike. We need more of this in the world today. We need more people saying, I do not like this...it is hard for me to stomach, but I will let go of trying to control it, of trying to make it what *I* think it should be, and trying to force *my* will on it. So many things happen today that are truly shocking with politics being one of the biggest. For some reason, people think that if they do not like someone or something, then they have the right to tear it down, to destroy it, put their hands on someone else, or worse end it forever. I feel badly for people are both intolerant and unaccepting, because they are blind. They lack faith. They rely solely on themselves, and if I stop a moment and vibe on some in particular in the news lately…. they are listening to darker angels. This is quite easy, because when you have no faith in a higher power, it is easier for the darker things to send the messages. If you are not hearing positive messages that lift you and others up...then they are not coming from a higher power with your best interests at heart.

Acceptance, not tolerance will make this world a better place to live in now and later for children and grandchildren. Acceptance means that you love the person with the nose ring and purple hair. Acceptance means that you love others above all else. So hard to do, but anything is possible when you weigh yourself against your own heart and not the hearts of others. I am just given this and will write it before I forget it....and remember that courage and bravery only rise when fear is present. Courage and bravery come from God. When you feel the need, that means you are meant to overcome something. Fear may be present to stop you, but fear comes from.... well, you figure it out.

God grant me the serenity to accept the things I cannot change, the courage to change the things I can, and the wisdom to know the difference.

-Reinhold Niebuhr

YOUR RELATIONSHIP WITH GOD

This is a short, sweet chapter on your relationship with God. Some have an excellent, church-driven and supported relationship, some are more private about their relationship, and others have none at all. I don't know how those people survive, but that is not my business. Regardless of how you relate to Spirit, having a connection is incredible and is what you want to make it. I for one enjoy sitting on a bench by a lake, resting my head on Jesus' lap while he tells me all the good I did during the day, as well as giving me instructions for improvement. These conversations are very important to my spiritual growth, as I am only human and mess up constantly. Thank God He's the forgiving type. Kind of like…. shaking His head at me and rolling His eyes at my stupidity, and yet proud of me when I do good. Just like any parent. Yes…just like any parent.

Let me start off by saying that your relationship with God is the same as your relationship with your own parents, and it may even mimic your reliance on Him or your desire to stand alone and do it all by yourself. I guess if you felt pushed away or made to do more on your own that you might feel less of an inclination to rely on or give so much of your life to another entity…but I do, because God has never failed me. I give Him everything, because when no one else if listening, He does, and then He gives it to me straight…I know that His advice and guidance is not biased, or tainted, or hurtful, or judgmental, rather it is to help me whether I like or understand it. My dog was a great listener for a long time, and she was the same way; however, she didn't give me great advice, simply looked at me and aske me to rub her belly.

Let me give you some more instances here….

God simply wants to be there for you just as any parent wants to be there for their children. I don't care what religion you practice, whomever you pray to, all the same God anyway, when you talk to God, you are talking to your Heavenly Father. I know as a mother that I want my kids to come to me with anything, and then hopefully, I will be able to love them enough to give them good advice without injecting my personal will into it. My kids know that I will love them and support them regardless of who they love, how they love, or what they choose to do with their lives, as long as it is legal and builds character, and I say this confidently, because God loves all of His children the same, regardless of their color, race, choice of love, or sin. He is unconditional in the way He loves, and so I choose to be. Please remember that religious books, as true as they may be, were interpretations of God's Word, and thus infused with political agendas, human fears and perspectives of those times, so saying that God does not love all of His children because of their sexual identity or religious affiliation, or for being a spirit seeing medium is crazy. Those are men's fears, not God's….as He does not fear.

So…back on track here…You go through life and you wonder why things have gone to hell in a handbasket, wondering who can help you through trials and tribulations. The only answer I can give you is Father God. If you open your mind and soul enough to listen to His answers, you might find yourself arguing with Him that you don't want to do what he suggests because it is too hard, or that you think His answer is stupid, but you know it's the right thing to do. Believe me, arguing with 'self' is one step closer to having a better relationship with God, because those 'conversations' or talking to self is one way for Him to reach you. But as I have stated before, ONLY listen to the good, positive things that lift you and others up higher.

Now, remember where you stand. I have talked about God tying your shoes, and this is very true. If you want His help, then you must ask for it and then remove yourself and your will from the equation or else you get in His way. Let Him work for you, because He will gladly do it if you stop trying so hard to do it yourself. With that in mind I will tell you this story. God has a funny way of infusing little gems of lessons into my life to help me better understand things. One day I was sitting on my daughter's bedroom floor and she was getting dressed. She asked me to button her shirt for her. I said, Sure, come here and I will do it for you. She said, come here and do it, and I replied, No, you come here! I'm not moving. I was simply not moving for her. If she needed my help, she could come to me. She walked over and as I was trying to button her shirt, she kept leaning backwards and pulling out of my hands. I said, Stop moving away! Do you want me to button your shirt or not? And BAM! it hit me. God doesn't move…we do.

He is stationary, always sitting in the same place, but we wander away, we ask for help, but we lean the other way. On purpose? Defiantly? No. We simply do it. My daughter wasn't being bad or defiant, she was simply being a child and in her own thoughts. For me it was a wake up that God does not move, we do. All you have to do is go to Him and allow Him to work in your life, be it buttoning your shirt or tying your shoes…. Let Him do what He can.

I can honestly say that I try to love everyone, but sometimes my human feelings kick in and I decide how to feel based on human feelings rather than spiritual feelings. I believe the spiritual influence is much stronger at overcoming dislike of situations, people, and other things, because it allows us to feel and ultimately see people and situations as God sees then rather than as a human judges them. I like it better that way, but it is not always easy. As I have already said, I find it difficult sometimes giving someone the benefit of the doubt when they are simply outright nasty. I find it easier to ignore them rather than play nice. I do not want to be a hypocrite or two-faced so until I can come around to something or someone, I simply stay clear. I ask God for His help and guidance, and funny enough, He has provided me with the means of helping people that has actually backfired on me at times, simply by opening up to someone with love and forgiveness only to find that they do not feel like doing the same. I know when to cut off my losses and move on. Giving people the benefit of the doubt is great, but not to your own detriment. Know when to walk away and call the play.

The saying What would Jesus do, is something I *do* ask myself once in a while, when I feel my judgement is off. I ask this because I want to make the best decision, and it may be that the best decision is not what I would humanly want to do. Remember, I AM human, and I make selfish choices once in a while, and I make choices that may not be best, so I ask…What would Jesus do? If you are ever at a loss for knowledge or discernment, simply ask for help. If you are wondering wear God went, then go look for Him. If you are wondering where He was when something bad happened, then you need more understanding of how God works…. He does not allow or condone bad things, but again, He cannot affect free will. Consider your parents on this.   All parents can do is their best to raise solid, upstanding citizens of society. Eventually children move out and run free, to be on their own. During that time, we can only hope our children will do well. There are times when you must watch your child fail and there is nothing you can do about it. But parents are always there no matter what their children do, most of the time unconditionally, ready to help any way they can. This is not always true but is true for the most part. I said it before, that parents will unconditionally love their children no matter the crime, and this is how God loves each of His children.

LETTING GO & FORGIVENESS

One of the hardest things that you can ever do is to forgive someone. Let's not even consider someone else, just consider forgiveness of self. It is not something that we do neither with ease nor readily. Forgiveness is not just something most people can do or provide, forgiveness may come in time, or after a lot of contemplation. Regardless, forgiveness comes from faith and the belief that you do not need to hold onto pain, frustration, hurt, or loss; rather, you can give it all up to God and be on your way.

Sometimes we hear of something tragic happening, like a child being murdered, only to hear months later in the news that the family forgave the person who committed the crime. I know that I have thought to myself, "Am I capable of forgiving someone of such an act? Would I be capable of letting go so much as not to judge that person or condemn them to hell?" I would hope that my faith is strong enough that I would, yes, still be angry, but also to be able to have enough compassion to ask myself why this person felt it was okay to commit this crime; I would hope that my faith is strong enough not to condemn that person. Now I'm no hypocrite, and there are people that I judge right off the cuff based on, let's say, something that they say or do. But, don't get me wrong... I always step back, and think, "Was that a proper judgment, or is there more to this story?" I always try to give someone a chance.

It can be very tough in today's world to put things aside, however, if we are here to grow spiritually and become better people...then forgiveness is a lesson that we all must learn. So, does forgiveness come in time, or is it something that we just automatically give? I will, also, say that throughout my life I have always immediately forgiven people for things that they have done to me. As a child, I found myself constantly apologizing to people about things I had never even done, but I merely wanted their friendship, and I would say, "I'm sorry, I don't know what I did, but I'm sorry for whatever it was." I would also forgive everyone all the time, and never hold a grudge against them. I'm still like that in many ways, and I even usually always give the benefit of the doubt when people mistreat me. Again, don't get me wrong - I might think you're a complete jerk - but I will always be kind.

Not to get off track, but some stories must be shared. I've been doing this a long time and what I have found is that we are told not to judge. It repeatedly states that in the Bible and other religious artifacts that *we are not to judge*. What people don't understand is that judgment does not stop at others' feet. If you are judging others, then you most likely judge yourself as well. People wake up in the morning immediately judging themselves. They look in a mirror, and they think, "I'm too fat, my hair is too straight or too thin or too kinky, my butt is too big or too small, I have cellulite, I have a birthmark, I have a big nose, I have buck teeth, I have yellow teeth, I am not good enough, my boobs are too small, my boobs are too big, I'm too tall, I'm too short, I'm too fat!" I don't have to go on because I can guarantee that while you're reading this, those things that you say to yourself every day are already on your tongue.

Judging self is usually quite effortless. I will tell you that the darker things like it when we judge ourselves because when we do that we feed into self-defeat, self-deprecation, and belittling, all of which feed into self-demolition. Judging ourselves comes easy and is quick. The darker things enjoy this because when we judge ourselves to be a bad person, or to think the wrong things, or to want something that society does not agree with, they take those indifferences and run with them, leaving us with the feeling that we are horrible people. Now, why would they do that? Because when we are self-defeated, and when we are constantly hearing the negatives *about* our self, *from* our self, they have a better chance at winning. Loud voices are hard to ignore…… and these voices are loud.

Let me explain the importance of not judging yourself and forgiving yourself for being human. When we die, we go where we believe we should go. We don't go where God judges us to go; I know, because I have seen murderers in heaven who have accepted things that they've done and realized they were wrong. So, look at it this way: You have just died, and you're being pulled through a tunnel. Suddenly you start thinking to yourself all the things that you did in life that were bad, or that you deemed wrong. The next thing you know, you're being pulled towards the darkness, not a Heavenly, loving light, but rather darkness, and an emptiness. Judging oneself means that you will condemn yourself, so don't do it. If you can offer yourself forgiveness and believe that in doing so you are giving your pain to God, then *that is true forgiveness.*

Find a way to forgive people, including yourself, and let go of the burden of carrying hate, anger, and loathing, because honestly, what we feel about others has an impact on us, as well, like throwing mud at a mirror. What?! Picture a bucket full of all the feelings you have for someone who has hurt you. Create a sludge of tears, pain, regret, fear, hate, and upset; swirl it around into a repulsive pool of septic nastiness. Watch the slurry curdle and bubble and turn black with resentment. The problem is that when you bring all these negative feelings together, you are cultivating and manifesting more of the same feelings. Dumping them on the person who has hurt you does no good because of their feelings in this matter...DO NOT MATTER. *You* are what matters here, and if you throw all the contents of that bucket on a person who may or may not care, you are essentially throwing your broken heart and soul away. The emotions in that bucket reflect yourself, and it does no good to throw them at the other person. Instead, acknowledge your feelings, see them for what they are, pull them out of you, and give them to God. See this happening and then do *not* listen to anything negative about yourself. Complete the task and wash off in white light like milk being poured over your head. This is good to do when in the shower because you can visualize and feel it flowing over you. You can then clarify your own behaviors, decide what is actually yours to deal with internally, and forgive and let go.

Look at the things that you've done in your life; consider all the circumstances around what you've done and ask yourself if were justified, or if you felt you were doing what was right at the time?

Consider who you are now, and would you, in your heart of hearts, do it again? A lot of people grow, and with growth, comes change; however, most people know right from wrong and behave as they believe they had to, given their circumstances or reputations. What I mean is that even though someone may feel one way or want to act a certain way, they instead behave in a way that is conducive to survival. For instance, a mother steals baby food to feed her child, she is arrested and booked for theft; however, what you don't know is that her husband is abusive and will not give her money, and the baby is hungry. She did what she had to do, not for herself, but for someone else. How can you judge someone when you don't know their story? Maybe a woman just walked into Walmart and stole $400 worth of clothes for the 10th time and got caught, yet again. What you don't know is that this is how she was raised, and having nothing growing up, coupled with a mother addicted to heroin, all while she was trying to protect her younger siblings, stealing became a way of earning mom's affection, as well as providing for her family. Now I am not saying everyone who has a sad story is justified for committing crimes, but what I *am* saying is that there is a story behind all actions, and without knowing the whole story, you condemn not only that person through judgment, but yourself as well.

God has a funny way of teaching us lessons when we condemn others out of ignorance.

Perspective and experience will make the same act different for everyone, but seeing the soul, rather than what earthly circumstances have pushed someone to think and behave a certain way, is the most amazing part of awakening; you start to see the beauty of everyone, regardless of their appearance or behavior, just as God sees each of us. It becomes easier to forgive, love, and accept others. So, to put it simply, don't judge. Consider the things that you have personally gone through, picture them, and then let them go. One of the ways that you can do this is by getting comfortable, and either sitting down in a chair or lying down in a comfortable area. Make sure you're not going to be bothered by your cell phone or TV or a knock on the door. Next, think of the things that have happened in your life that you judge yourself over. Maybe you yell at your kids too much. Perhaps you spoke too soon about something to someone. Maybe you had a bad attitude with someone, and you feel bad about it. Maybe you stole something, or committed a crime, and never turned yourself in. There are a lot of things that people hold against themselves, and the things that you consciously consider are what you are going to bring up in this exercise.

So, make sure you are laying down or sitting comfortably, and what you are going to do is close your eyes and see yourself in front of you. Maybe you are seven years old, or perhaps you're the age you are now. You are going to look at yourself and say, "I am sorry for putting you through this. I am sorry that I did these things." You are going to have a heart-to-heart discussion with yourself, either verbalizing your thoughts or doing it within your head. When you are done you are going to hug yourself, and you are going to hug yourself tight; you're going to see it, feel it, and you're going to experience it fully. Then, you're going to watch that 'self' walk away, and you're never going to think about it again. This is letting go and embracing the knowledge that your Father God still loves you.

Another cool way of letting go of something or forgiving self is through the cutting of cords. This is something I do all the time, especially if I find myself doing the dishes and I'm having a conversation in my head with someone. I realize I have some form of spiritual energy connection with this individual that I keep rehashing, and I need to let go of the person and situation altogether. Sometimes, if you find yourself talking to someone in your head, it's because they have a cord that is connected to you, as well. What I mean by cords is that we have "energy tentacles;" those tentacles are what reach out in a split-second to read people's energy, and then when we pull them back like a giant tongue, we see, feel, and sense what another person is about. We do it in split seconds and are able to read people's exuded energy. That is why the phrase, "Don't judge a book by its cover," is so famous. Also, sometimes what we sense is what the person is putting on for others to see initially, or for airs. If you really want an in-depth idea of a person, you must go talk to them, and peel back the first few layers so you can see them for who they truly are inside.

Cutting of the cords is quite simple. You will need the assistance of Archangel Michael, so at some point, you're going to have to have some form of belief that it's possible to talk to him. You will relax, not in a trance, but just naturally relaxed and open to the conversation. You will ask Archangel Michael to come down and be of assistance to you to cut cords of attachment from those things living dead or otherwise, that wish to do you harm. And you will ask Archangel Michael to take his glowing, electrified, blue sword and swipe down your left side, cutting cords of attachment from those things living dead or otherwise that wish to do you harm. And you will see all cords of different colors and strengths falling off you. You'll do the same for your right side, your front, your back, above your head, and below your feet, and with every swipe you will repeat those words. Then you will want to envision white light flowing through the top of your head and out the soles of your feet, enveloping you and protecting you. You want to finish off by making sure that all your own energy tentacles are pulled in, showing that you are whole. This is an excellent way to not only let go of energies that are painful but also to assess your own level of stress, in which case you will also be addressing your own voice and judgments of self and others.

Any kind of visualization that you do for healing may take time because the mind is attempting to change what the brain believes should be. Like I've written before, the brain processes what it knows, and the mind is open to suggestion, innovation, inventions, passions, determination, character, and all those things that cannot be measured. Ask a scientist to measure passion.... it can't be done with numbers and scales. Measuring feelings must be done through explanation, and that is why it's hard sometimes to forgive self and others. You can't put a number on it, and you can't say anything other than, it hurts like this or that. Consider doctor's offices having a scale from 1 to 10 with smiley faces and sad faces, because people can't numerically measure pain, hurt, judgment, and forgiveness, without being able to represent the actual feeling. So, when you are going through this process of cutting cords, and you start to pull your own energies back into yourself, just know that it may take some time and practice to learn how to reel yourself in, literally.

Let the truth be told, I am an emotional person, and I am also somebody who likes to talk about things right now. I do not like letting things linger, and I don't want energy just out there to be dispersed into the universe. I found myself in a situation of pain and upset, and the person with whom I was trying to have a conversation would not respond or talk to me. My hurt and pain and upset turned into a manifestation of anger, and subsequently, it came out that way, but it was also then coupled with stupidity. You can imagine that anger and stupidity are not qualities that need to mingle. That didn't stop me, and I let stupidity and anger flow from my mouth repeatedly. I don't believe that person ever spoke to me again. that doesn't mean that I haven't tried to make up for it, and apologize for being an ass, and although I still have the right to share my upset and hurt, I allowed my ego to get involved in the conversation. With that being said, I later had someone come to me requesting help in a situation that didn't truly involve or affect me. I was not going to play sides, and I honestly did not want to get involved; when I turned this person down, I received some very horrible and nasty messages and phone calls to the point where I had to block this individual from my life.

It then occurred to me that this person had done to me what I had done to the other, and I suddenly understood but that person would probably never speak to me again since I still could not find forgiveness for this individual that had attacked me. Know why can't I forgive them? Well, in the Bible it says you should forgive someone repeatedly - 77 times, to be exact - which means you should always forgive, and for many years I had forgiven this person because I had identified her early on as the Scorpion. which made me wonder if this guy had ever identified me with an animal. I have yet to ever speak to her again because I also believe that you must cut toxic people from your life: so maybe he sees me as toxic. But I can't be angry at him because I understand. The point being that regarding both situations, I forgive him for never talking to me again, I forgive myself for being the ass in that relationship, and I forgive her for being a scorpion, but only because I'm compassionate to her situation. I have no need for scorpions.

Now you ask what do you mean by a scorpion? Well, having compassion for someone means that you have looked at their situation and you are attempting to understand what they have gone through, and are therefore willing to allow them into your life at a certain level and point. This does not mean that you are going to entirely, 100% trust someone whom you know has committed certain acts that you find disagreeable. It means that you are willing to allow someone into your life, and you keep them within the distance that you know that you remain safe. There are people within my life that I look at and think that person is a snake, or that person is a scorpion, and what I mean is that their true nature, regardless of how they are one day, may eventually come through. By being aware of a person's true nature, I prevent myself from getting into an ill-situation with that individual as well as preventing myself from getting hurt. By hurt, I mean both emotionally damage, as well as not expecting so much. Where that old friend of mine is concerned, for many years I viewed her as a scorpion because I knew that if I got too close to her that she would hurt me. So, I didn't have an expectation of her being any other way (oh, and I, also, was not the victim and I did not get hurt when her true side came through). Eventually, she was going to sting me, and she tried many times. I forgave her for those many attempts; but, ultimately, it got to a point where I was just tired of trying to avoid the sting.

Consider the people in your life right now and think of those that you know for sure are the ones that you can trust with your life. Also, consider those around you who you must be aware of and more on your toes, and then decide how many more times you will forgive them or give them the benefit of the doubt or try to fix the situation. Because even Jesus knew when to quit. What I mean is that you must be aware of and understand your limit for your own well-being. Know when to let go of things you cannot change. This leads me to forgive others as well as self, through a process of visualization and meditation. It works because it causes you to let your guards down and helps to reveal your unconscious withholdings.

Picture a horse post, the kind they would tie horses to in the wild West. Now, envision all the people in your life whom you have had issues with, such as parents, siblings, employers, employees, other drivers or shoppers for that matter, neighbors, aunts, uncles, husband, wives, etc. Picture their faces as floating balloons and tie them all to the horse post. Start at one end of the post and see the person you are talking to floating in front of you. Say to that person, "I'm sorry, please forgive me, I love you, thank you," and see all that has transpired between you. See the pain, hurt, anger, passion, and feelings as they happened. This is called Ho'oponopono, and it is the release of energy, willfully and wholeheartedly. It is a release of both yours and the other person's power, and it is forgiveness. You may not forget what transpired, but you are letting go of what happened and the emotion, energy, and feelings that kept it locked tight to you. After you have said those words and after you have hugged that person...I don't care if they beat you daily...you perform this visual ritual, and you let them go. Untie their balloon and let it float away from you.

You will perform this visual exercise for every person tied to that post. You will see them, see what transpired between you both, and you will say, I'm sorry, please forgive me, I love you, thank you, and you will hug them and let them fly away. You will not attempt to grab them back or shoot them down; no matter how tempted you may be. ;) Finally, you will see yourself floating there in front of you. You will envision your life. You will see your happiness and your sadness. You will say, I'm sorry, please forgive me, I love you, thank you, and you will hug yourself.

The most amazing part of this process is the comprehension that what will be revealed to you are the very things that you have unintentionally or unconsciously held against yourself. Things that you did not even know were still festering will be brought to your attention and you will finally have a chance to mend hurt and repair wounds. Things you never knew existed within your heart, mind, and soul will be brought to the surface. Cry like a baby; cradle yourself and love yourself, finally... after all this time. Let yourself just go. It is an amazing, snotty, blurry, ugly cry, but it is so fulfilling and awakening.

Forgiving others is refreshing and can help remove anxiety as well. It takes away that lump in the pit of your stomach, because most of the time, the only power we have is to forgive. And forgiving does not mean the person gets away with something, but rather they lose your attachment, and you walk away with less burden of maintaining that upset, anger, hurt, frustration, or pain. Don't forget hate, because hate is a very compelling word, let alone feeling the urge to continually manifest that hate at the drop of someone's name.

Believe me, there are people I feel that passionate about, but when I find myself saying, "I hate..." something or someone, I stop and reconsider my feelings and words. Let me show an example.... I am going to think of someone, and instead of saying I hate them, I am going to clarify my feelings as...loathe the way they behave. I am sure this

This is a vision of someone letting go of their pain, regret, hurt, suffering, and anger. She is envisioning all those who have hurt her and who she has hurt in the forms of balloons. She then says to each person, 'I'm sorry. Please forgive me. I love you. Thank you,' and unties them. She lets them float away, untying herself from them forever. Her energy as a little girl is there to comfort her from all she has punished herself for and is now realizing and letting go.

person does not deserve to be hated, and I must find the source of energy to offer this person understanding or compassion.

Oh, how easy it is to thumb my nose at this person and just be as rude back; however, what would that prove? Nothing. I must control my own behavior, and by being a jerk back to this individual would mean that person was controlling me...not going to happen if I can help it. Forgiveness means compassion and understanding, two things we are not born with. We must learn forgiveness and understanding and accept them, allowing them to flow through us.

Understanding someone does not just simply happen because you choose to follow them. Understanding only occurs when you open yourself up to see what that person may have lived or how they would have walked. Knowledge and understanding only comes with compassion, and compassion only comes when you are open to Spirit working within you. When you ask yourself why someone acts the way they do, it may be because they do cannot open themselves up to allowing Spirit To flow through them. They may not have the ability to believe that they could be a vessel for Spirit to work through; for this I pity people. For this reason, I am writing this book, in the hopes that people will see themselves in some of these scenarios and open themselves to the idea that there is more to us than skin and bones.

Speaking of skin and bones, the Bible says ashes to ashes and dust to dust and that eventually, we will all go back to the ground where we came from. And so that leads me to another way of letting go. Envision the problem, regardless of what it is, such as an argument, or a fight or a simple daily stressor, and put it in your hand so that you can see it in a holographic form. Look at it, acknowledge what it is, and understand all the emotions and feelings that go with that situation scenario or person. While you are envisioning all of that mustered together, identify where in your body those feelings are coming from. If it's anger and you feel it in your throat, pull that dark energy from your throat. If it's frustration and it's coming from your hands, draw the dark energy from your hands. If it's sadness and it's coming from your stomach, pull that dark energy from your gut and pile the whole of it up on top of the situation you are holding in your hand. Then you will see that pile in your hand to a pyre, watch the flames rise and devour the entire case in its entirety; watch the smoke rise to the heavens, and watch it be enveloped and accepted into the sky. What is left in your hand is the Earthly evidence of that problem, manifested as ashes in the palm of your hand. Finally, gently and lovingly blow the ashes out of your hand and scatter them to the wind.

The biggest lesson that I want everyone to be aware of is that when you hold on to upset, anger, frustration, or hate, *they do manifest within your body*. You may see that your daily stressors settle in your shoulders, and by the end of the day, you have a raging headache. You may find that your stressors settle in your stomach or in your intestines and the slightest binge of fat or grease, or anything for that matter, set your gut into a wretched mess. You may find that your stressors settle in your back and by the end of the day you can barely walk, which over time could turn into sciatica, which then reaches down the back of your leg, behind your knee, and then to your ankles. Your stressors may be of the heart, and you may be carrying a burden of upset, hurt, and pain from what happened when you were a child, as it may have been a great and grand sadness that sliced your heart in half. Sometimes people do not have a chance to work through those problems, or they just don't know how; maybe they just don't want to. Those stressors that affect the heart spiritually will eventually affect your heart physically. Why? Because they are underlying, and they affect your happiness, your perceptions, your perspectives, how you give of yourself and how you receive others.

You may not realize it, but the pains that affect your heart, affect how you love, accept, and how you allow yourself to be loved. Emotional stressors *do* manifest and *do* physically affect you; therefore, it is so important to address your emotional upsets.

Put it this way... if you are constantly struggling with emotional issues, they create in the human body hormones, such as cortisol or adrenaline, and those can be scientifically measured to cause physical disabilities and imbalances. Medical doctors and scientists alike will agree that chronic hormonal imbalances and cortisol issues, coupled with adrenaline rushes and anxiety can cause physical disability long term. The thing is that when the body sees itself as the culprit, or the one causing all the problems, it will turn on itself. And so, you may have nothing other than a palpitation, or just feeling tired all the time and then suddenly bam, you're hit with lupus or chronic fatigue. The body will turn on itself and that is why it is so important to address forgiveness, your innermost feelings, letting go, and finding a means to relax and to breathe until love.

The process of forgiving and letting go is not so much for the other person as it is for you. We carry a lot of burdens anyway...things that we are fully aware of. So why would we attempt to carry things that exist within our energy, but do not make themselves truly known until they manifest as a disease or autoimmune issue? Addressing emotional and spiritual issues and pain is just as important as seeing a doctor for a stuffy nose or pain in your side. Treating the issue itself will prevent more health problems from manifesting. By letting go, truly letting go of some painful memory or feeling can help you heal in many ways. And it can prevent more physical maladies from developing.

Mind, body, and spirit = One Being, so do not neglect one aspect of who you are this life.

STORIES SHARED

Many people want to share their stories about how their readings affected their lives. I am offering two stories from individuals who have strong stories to tell, and who believe that the messages they received helped them move through a terrible time in their lives. Having hope, finding comfort, and learning you have more strength than you originally believed are not bad outcomes. Here are true-life stories from Anna O. and Patti S., both of whom have touched my life with their courage and grace.

ANNABELL'S STORY

April 5th, 2017 was the day my whole world stopped, and I remember that day so clearly. It was the day I lost my son, and nothing would ever be the same.

Hunter had school that day and afterwards he had some appointments that we needed to go to. We took my truck and I let him drive but he was in a hurry because he wanted to get home and he wasn't being very nice to me, short tempered and snappy. He liked to try to text and drive, always trying to be sneaky about it. After I caught him a couple of times, I told him he was grounded, for one week he had to be home by 9 pm. If there's one thing Hunter hated it was having to be home early and he was upset with me for that. He was such a momma's boy. He always told me that the loved me every day with a hug and a kiss too. My husband would say that I babied Hunter too much and maybe that was a little true, but Hunter was usually always grateful and even though he may not have liked it, he tried to follow the rules. But this day there were no hugs, or I love you's as he walked out our front door for the final time, on his way to see his girlfriend Bailey. It was his way of showing me he was mad. If I would have known that Hunter was going home to God that night, I would have held him tight, not let him leave. I would have hugged that last, I love you out of him and maybe if he would have known he would have had a different attitude to me as well.

Night came, and Hunter hadn't come home, he was late. I texted Bailey and she said he'd left a while ago because he didn't want to be late. In my heart I knew something was wrong. It was a "mom" instinct. It was like my heart stopped. I called my husband Jack, who was working in North Dakota and told him what I was feeling. He could tell by my voice that something wasn't right with me. Although he tried, Jack couldn't reach Hunter either.

I live across from the fire department and I remember watching them quietly back out of the station and then take off like a bat out of hell south out of town. It's a small town. They knew who was in the accident and I believe they were trying to be discreet, but I knew it was Hunter. I knew it was my son. Jack was still on the phone. He told me to get our other son, Josh, up to take me to follow the fire trucks and ambulance. When I went to get Josh, he was up like a shot, never questioning me or arguing with me, something he's prone to doing. He knew by my tone something was wrong.

Hunter's accident happened about 5 miles south of our home on a little county road. According to the police report they figured he lost control of the vehicle when he came up on a small curve in the road. A curve he'd taken a hundred times before. The PT Cruiser he was driving flipped several times and Hunter was ejected almost 90 feet from the vehicle. He was not wearing his seat belt but even if he would have it probably wouldn't have mattered. The cruiser was flattened. I wanted more answers but there weren't any. There were no witnesses, no cameras, no pictures, just the law enforcement's speculations. Could a deer have jumped out from the neighboring river timber and startled him? Could he have been texting while he was driving? As I sat in the emergency room with my dying son, my 4 other children and my husband still hanging on the phone, temporarily forgotten by his daughter, I realized it didn't matter. Everything was surreal. This could not be happening to me, to us, to our family. My daughter Sierra finally realized that her father was still on the phone and she found the strength to do the unimaginable. She told her dad that Hunter wasn't going to pull through this while he tried to deny the inevitable, telling her she was wrong, they just needed get him to a bigger hospital he argued. He went silent for a moment trying to reconcile what everyone else was already acknowledging. Then, in the darkest and lowest voice my daughter had ever heard from her father, Jack told her to put the phone to my ear. Our children stood around us as we broke down and I held the phone to Hunters ear, so Jack could say goodbye to his youngest child from the seat of his semi somewhere in the darkness of North Dakota.

A doctor asked us if we wanted a priest Hunter was given his last rites. It wasn't a priest that Hunter knew but it was someone to help Hunter make the journey into the Lord's arms. As they disconnected the monitors and machines from Hunter the lines beeped and went flat. It was over. Quietly and respectfully, knowing how raw we all were, a nurse and another lady asked if Hunter was an organ donor, what funeral home we would like to use and just like that the process of burying my child had begun. One by one I told my children to go home, I wanted to be alone. I needed to be alone. As I sat there hugging my dead son waiting for the coroner to come, I knew that this would be the longest night of my life. I finally drove myself home in the early morning hours and when I got home, I opened the first of several beers drinking myself into an exhausted sleep feeling alone and heartbroken.

The next days and weeks were a blur. Jack drove home overnight, stopping once overcome with grief for his lost child. When he made it home, we went out to the accident site as a family, where we cried and held each other. Trying to make sense of it all, looking to see if we could find clues the police could not. There were arrangements to be made. Visitors, too many to count, hugs and tears, people who came by and helped pull a feeling of organization out of the loss and chaos. Food was delivered, and Hunters friends held vigil on the front lawn trying to cope with their new-found knowledge that youth is not granted a free pass from death. One of the kids had been talking about the Texting and Driving Awareness that Humboldt had just done at the fairground. They thought it was funny and a little stupid. It wasn't so funny or stupid anymore. Reality had hit home.

Jack and I still had to bury our baby boy accidents require an autopsy, which meant we had to wait 5 days before we could bury Hunter and it seemed like a lifetime. Memories are disjointed. I remember everything, at least I think I do, but it seems to come back in pieces. A sea of faces, condolences, phone calls, flowers, memorials and then the funeral itself. Having to say a final goodbye to Hunter as he lay in his casket at the back of the church. Not wanting to, knowing that this was the last time I would see his face or brush his hair with my hand. I watched his brother and sisters say their final goodbyes. My husband had to half drag and carry me away from Hunter and down the church aisle to the seating reserved for the immediate family. My heart was surely broken.

One of the biggest challenges I had that day, knowing I had to leave Hunter in the ground at that cemetery, was questioning if there truly is a God or if God really did take him "home". I've always had faith that there is a God and that there is a Heaven or a final reward for God children but having to deal with all of this was a challenge for me. It was true test of my faith. I was never mad at God though. I believe when it is your time, it's your time but it didn't stop me from crying until my body was so exhausted that I would just sleep. I started praying and asking God to please forgive me and everything I did because I wanted to be able to be there and see Hunter again.

Days drug by. A week after we buried Hunter, we had our 1st holiday without him. Easter, celebrating the death of Christ and his resurrection, the irony was not lost on me, but I was trying to put on a brave face, trying to remember that I had other children and grandchildren that needed me. I couldn't seem to pull myself out of the dark depression that Hunter's death had put me in. I was prisoner of my own emotions. I knew that Hunter wouldn't have wanted me to feel this way but as Spring turned into

Summer I kept finding reminders of Hunter all around me. At one point I'd even thought of suicide, but I knew I couldn't because if there is a God and the Bible is the truth then killing myself wouldn't get me to Heaven. I couldn't do that because then I would NEVER see Hunter again and I couldn't do that.

A few months after Hunters death I realized I was still struggling with the question of God and Heaven. Is it real? I needed answers, to know that he was ok. As parents we always make sure we tell our children to let us know that they made it home or wherever they're going but I wasn't going to get a text from Hunter saying, "I'm here". At least I didn't think I was until one of my sweet friends Brenda M. messaged me

and told me about Rebecca Foster. Brenda thought maybe I should reach

out to Rebecca and maybe she could help me find answers I was so

desperately seeking. I was scared to even reach out at first, but I

reminded myself to keep my mind open, so I took the 1st step and sent

Rebecca a brief message that I had recently lost my son, and someone

had told me to contact her. She quickly responded to say no more that

she wanted to "channel" me and then she would get back to me. Several

days went by and before Rebecca contacted me and when she did, she

said that she saw a young boy who had died at a young age. She said this

boy made the shape of a heart. Perhaps this was his way of saying he

loved me. She then mentioned something about swords but that I should

already know what that was. I wasn't sure what to think of that but later I

looked up the meaning of a sword and I found this "And take... the

sword of the Spirit, which is the word of God" (Ephesians 6:17). Hunter

then presented her with the image of him plopping down on a brown

couch like a basement couch, put is feet up and gave a big cheesy smile.

He made a point of showing her his smile. Yes, we had a couch in our

basement and yes it was brown.

Then Hunter presented information to Rebecca about his accident. Crossing his chest. Next, he wanted Rebecca to acknowledge for his dad him putting on a baseball cap and swinging a bat. Rebecca said he came through with nothing but love happiness and reassurance. He mentioned his big toe for whatever reason, which might seem odd to some people but the night of Hunters accident his big toe was pretty torn up. She let me know that Hunter seemed like a normal happy teenager plopping down on a couch making himself at home. Rebecca got the impression from Hunter that his "Heaven" is his home where he lived with me, so he had created his Heaven to be squishy like his home.

She then went into great detail about how Hunter was coming home and missed the curve that was going left and underestimated it because he was not focused on the road. She said that Hunter was expressing that he had only looked down for a second. She was able to describe the scene of the accident as if she had been there. She got so into detail that's when Jack and I truly started to believe in her. It was as if she was in the car with him. She talked about the wheels catching the edge of the road and he overcorrected going into the ditch sideways or rolling. She also said that Hunter said as crazy as it was it was his time and fully accepts it and he's OKAY. He told Rebecca that he was going to do good things on the other side while everyone else he loves is still here. Rebecca reassured me that Hunter is always here by my side when he gets the chance and should look for signs. I believe that because I swear, I can feel him, his presence, at times around me.

Rebecca does a lot of online readings, so I would watch for her and get online hoping to hear something from Hunter. There are several things that Hunter has brought across to Rebecca that there is no way for her to know unless Hunter's presence is conveying it to her. Sometimes if Hunter wants to really get across to me, Rebecca will reach out and let me know. Sometimes the messages are just to make me laugh. She talks about his big cheesy smile and him being a jokester with a big heart. These messages are a blessing because even though he is no longer here on earth I can still communicate with him in the afterlife. I know from these messages that Hunter IS in Heaven and at peace which gives me some peace and comfort. Sometimes I feel crazy trying to explain to people how I have accepted and come to terms with what has happened. Some people just don't understand, and I truly feel sorry for them. There are many parents I'm sure who have struggled with the same questions I did. They've lost a child and don't know if that child's spirit is ok. I know this taunt them just as it did me and I've heard this from several parents as well.

Rebecca has helped me heal. At first, I felt like I was almost harassing Rebecca because that first little glimpse of Hunter was the biggest gift, I've ever received so naturally I wanted more but I didn't understand that wasn't always going to happen. I had to understand that if Hunter had a message for me, he would get it to me in good time. Rebecca has an amazing gift and I thank God for her. I believe in my heart that God answered my prayers though Rebecca Foster. Without her spiritual guidance and help I don't think I would be where I am today. I can now find the joy in life again. I spend time cuddling and loving my grandbabies, cherishing them and finding all the blessings around me.

I thank God for the 17 &1/2 years that he blessed us with Hunter. I feel almost lucky for that much time with him. There are so many parents that lose their children at even younger ages. I got to know my son through all his stages of life, babyhood, toddle, pre-teen, teenager as he grew into a young man. He was such a gift from God, and I am grateful for all the memories I have of Hunter.

Annabelle and Hunter

My life forever changed on April 5th, 2017 and yes it will never be the same as it once was, but I have found a way to go forward, finding peace and comfort in the realization that even though we may lose those who we love they have not lost us. Their presence is always with us.

I am thankful for Rebecca helping in the way that no one else could and I hope that my story can help others find the answers or solace from Rebecca that I was able to find.

God Bless.

Love

Annabell O.

~~~~~~

PATTI'S STORY

I would like to start out by saying that when I met Rebecca, I was going thru some very dark times. I wasn't sure what was happening to me. She told me it was a depression (That I was IN the water.) At that time, I didn't know how far that depression would take me. Things were happening to me that I couldn't understand, and I didn't know how to ask anyone about what to do about it.

The man I knew as my father was dying of cancer, my children were dealing with their own issues, and so much was changing that I couldn't keep up. My job was awful, and Rebecca tried and tried to tell me to leave and do something else, but I couldn't find my way out of there. It's funny how God works too. Ya know what He did: Lol, He closed the office down! hahaha God does have a way of getting us to do what HE wants us to do, huh? :) What a Blessing that turned out to be for me!

During a reading with Rebecca, I was asking what I should do with myself now. She told me about Reiki, and said I needed to look into it. I had never in my life heard of that before though, but I found someone close by that taught my daughter Virginia and me to be Reiki Masters. That changed my life. So many things started to make sense to me! I understood why I would get so tired or out of sorts when I was in a crowd of people (empath, energy).

I remember one of our first meetings I wasn't so much wanting a reading as I was wanting to know how Rebecca did what she did. I asked her if she saw things with your eyes or if in your mind, or if she heard voices inside or outside of her head? lol

Or if she just "knew" things. Sometimes I myself just "know" things and couldn't explain why I knew them. No one ever talked about that stuff and when I would bring it up people would think I was nuts. I guess I really needed a mentor. Lol. I thought I found one with Kathy, the woman who taught us reiki, but that didn't turn out so good...

Kathy did explain to me that what I call my depression was me "waking up," which made perfect sense to me.

On one visit I had with Rebecca, she said I would have a scare with breast cancer and to not worry about it, because it would all be ok. And guess what? She was totally right! When Virginia graduated high school, I found a lump in my breast. It was removed and found to be much larger than they first thought, but all was well as it was not cancer. Jump forward a few years, and on the other breast I had a black discharge that had cancer cells in it. So, I had to have the milk ducts removed on that side. I was not afraid because Rebecca told me it would all be ok. And it was. :) THANK YOU, Rebecca, for that. :)

Rebecca warned me about my husband Kevin's heart too. She said it was bad and he needed to have it checkout. But right around that time Kevin had had a scare at work where he passed out. It was determined to be some infection around his heart (pleurisy?) and I thought that was what she was referring to, but nope... it was worse than that. Time went on and he recovered from the infection. But he was to have surgery on his wrist for carpel tunnel and that's when they found out about his heart being really, bad. That was back in 2009 when he got the defibrillator put in. Rebecca was right on the money as far as Kevin and his heart were concerned! Thank you for the heads up too!!

I also remember when she said she needed to see Virginia. She would have been about 17 years old at the time. Poor girl was really going thru some stuff that I was uncapable of helping her with. Sitting at your kitchen table Rebecca asked her how long she had been hearing the voices and seeing dead people. Her face turned beet red and she looked at me. I had NO idea she was experiencing those things. I had no idea how to help her. Growing up I would 'poopoo" things away that she would tell me. Like the guy standing in her doorway at night that only she could see. She never told me about him till later. But we did find out he was her guide and was just protecting her at night while she slept. ;) That meeting with Virginia helped to bring us closer together too. Rebecca also told me to listen to Virginia when she would tell me things and I want her to know, I do! Lol. That is probably the biggest blessing

Rebecca gave me.... helping me to understand my daughter. I thank her for that. :)

Rebecca has been such a blessing in my life.

Thank you for everything you do lady!

God Bless you and yours,

Patti

A.L.'S INPUT & VISUAL

My most recent reading with Dr. Foster describes my awakening, all the way down to shedding my old, worn, graffiti-stained skin, and becoming my new self as my new skin envelops around me. Just the day before, I had told a friend that I wished I could just take my skin off and replace it with new. So many things in my life this year has been a shedding of the old, and a building of the new; I am preparing to be woke, even in this dimension.

~ A. L.

I did a reading on A.L. and the vision of her walking towards a doorway all lit up and shining on her was there. As she walked closer, I could see her skin, all tattered, beaten, scarred, labeled...falling off of her. She was taking her skin off and stepping into a whole new way of being. The realization that this is simply an earthly skin was the message, and that she was healing, walking towards the energy, the light.... she was healing. That light can very well be positive thinking and belief in self.

These are just a few of the stories I shared because they show pain and growth, healing, and discovery. I hope they reach those reading.

EPILOGUE

It has taken me a long time to decide to write this book and then a long time to put it together…years in fact, because I did not have the time or energy that I knew would be needed to complete it. During my writing process I had a conversation with someone who helped give me direction, and he made my reason for writing it even more meaningful. I knew after our conversation that this book was meant to reach as many people as possible without barrier, and that I had to get it into as many hands as possible….and that is all that mattered. While I was writing I envisioned the pages being passed on from friend to friend, family member to family member as they saw themselves and their loved ones described in the pages. I saw their faces change as they read a sentence that hit home, smack right in the soul. My intentions as I wrote were to give people just one moment that made them stop and think, and ponder their situations, and consider the similarities, and how could someone else possibly know what they were going through? I wanted to make a difference and shed some hope on others' lives.

One thing to remember as you finish this book is that everyone has a story that they can tell about an experience that was happy, sad,

painful, crucial, thoughtful, and exhilarating. What people don't realize
is that we all have similar lessons, it's just that the lessons are
incorporated differently based on the environment and experiences
relative to each individual. We all have jobs, we all love, we all hate, we
all dislike, figure, coerce, befriend, enable, take care of, soothe, minister,
rise, fall, accept, tolerate, win and lose. We all do the same things, yet
people want to consider all the appearance differences, the life
differences, but must understand that we have lived many lives…and
those you dislike now, tolerate now, hate now, fight now, etc., are
probably whom you lived as at one time. Keep in mind that we are
directed to love one another above all things, because love conquers a
multitude of sins. Love one another. It is very difficult to love everyone.
I know. But that is because we are human, and we tend to see the human
in people and not the spiritual. Try to think of one person whom you just
cannot bear to be around, and see them, feel what you feel about them,
but then, stand in front of them with God and look at that person with
your heart. What does God show you about that person? What does He
show you that goes beyond what you 'know?' Still hard. I know.
Attempt to look at people differently, but I will say this only comes with
compassion, and you must be open to compassion and vision or this

won't matter. I will add that I have seen people as human, and I have seen things shown to me, but it is still very hard to deal with them, because again, I am human, and it is easier to accept what you are shown and walk away rather than continue to put yourself in the position of getting hurt or upset. So, this exercise is for *you*, not them. It helps you to build a different perspective, maybe one of pity rather than hatred or disgust. Those are very heavy emotions to carry

My hope is that you enjoyed this book and what I have put into it. I hope you felt the energy that I put into this text and were able to make sense of the visuals. I hope that it made you consider more beyond this world that we live in. I hope it made you see that there is a world outside of this one that holds you tightly, embracing all your joys, all your upsets, and all your moments. I hope you see that you are loved by God and by many on the other side who work diligently to keep you happy, inspired, and moving forward. I hope that you found some answers, and I hope that maybe you found some relief as well. I can only trust that God will do what He wants to do with this book. I hope it reaches the people it is meant to reach.   Thank you for reading. God Bless.

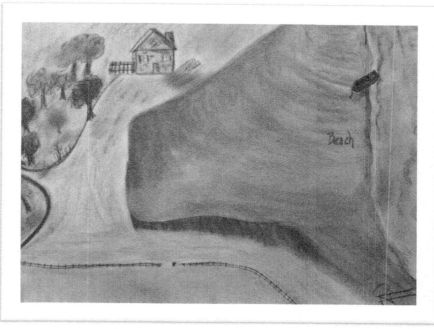

This is what the beach looks like to me from above. Each is specific to each individual, but this is the basic layout that I walk around every time I read for someone. Notice the sandy beach itself, the boat awaiting an opportunity, the path leading up with the field to the left where those passed meet up. On the left is the entrance to the forest, and beyond that is the house that represents the person for whom I am reading, along with the garden.

WHOOP WHOOP!!!!!!

A. FOX | EDITOR

A.Fox is a freelance editor, paralegal, and founder of an educational advocacy group. She has an extensive background in idiomology and language analysis with an emphasis on analytical dissemination of legal information.

BRIANNA SUTTON | ILLUSTRATOR

Brianna is a special education teacher for grades 4-6 at a rural elementary school. She lives in central Illinois and hopes to combine her passion for art with teaching special needs children. Music, dogs & cats, and ice cream are a couple other things she is unapologetically passionate about. More of Brianna's artwork can be seen on her Facebook page "Brianna Sutton's Art," or her personal Facebook page. To contact Brianna, use Facebook messenger or email her at Brianna.sutton@comcast.net

AUTHOR | ILLUSTRATOR | DR. REBECCA FOSTER

Email: rfoster8873@hotmail.com

Facebook: /GodsReader

Instagram: Midwest_Medium

Twitter: _RebeccaFoster

www.RebeccaFoster.Co

The End never really happens…